M
Gift

MONEY WISE

MONEY WISE

HOW TO CREATE, GROW, AND PRESERVE YOUR WEALTH

♦ ♦ ♦

A. MICHAEL LIPPER, CFA

DEVELOPER OF THE
LIPPER MUTUAL FUND INDICES

WITH DOUGLAS R. SEASE

ST. MARTIN'S PRESS ≈ NEW YORK

MONEY WISE. Copyright © 2008 by Whitridge LLC.
All rights reserved. Printed in the United States of America.
For information, address St. Martin's Press,
175 Fifth Avenue, New York, N.Y. 10010.

www.stmartins.com

Library of Congress Cataloging-in-Publication Data

Lipper, A. Michael.
    Money wise: how to create, grow, and preserve your wealth / by A. Michael Lipper, with
Douglas R. Sease.—1st St. Martin's Press ed.
        p. cm.
    ISBN-13: 978-0-312-37377-1
    ISBN-10: 0-312-37377-5
    1. Finance, Personal.   2. Investments.   3. Wealth.   I. Sease, Douglas.   II. Title.
    HG179.L523   2008
    332.024—dc22   2008009314

First Edition: September 2008

10 9 8 7 6 5 4 3 2 1

TO KAY

✦

✦ CONTENTS ✦

Contents

Part Two: APPROACHES TO INVESTING

Contents

A PERSONAL PREFACE

The Backstory on
Why This Book Was Written

As you will shortly learn, I come from a family that has successfully worked in Wall Street for four generations. While the various members of the family might well debate numerous things about the brokerage business, each would affirm and live by two interrelated principles. The first is that of a "due bill." Originally this was an additional piece of paper that was generated when certificates were exchanged between buyers and sellers. Often it noted that a payment of interest or a dividend would be forthcoming as soon as the certificates arrived at the selling firm and would be transmitted to the buying firm, which had legitimate claim to the income.

When Phil Revzin left Dow Jones to enter the book-publishing world, I inquired as to his plans, which led to a discussion of whether I would write a book for St. Martin's Press. I had been asked in the past by other publishers, but declined because they wanted books that would sell based on their promotional value such as *The Top Ten Mutual Funds to Buy Now* or *Fire Your Stockbroker, You Can Do It Yourself*. Phil asked me what kind of book I wanted to write. I said I wanted to write about the lessons that I had learned. Phil had been the publisher of *The Wall Street Journal Europe* at a critical time for my firm. Because of him we were able to get regular visibility in a major European publication. He assisted us in providing offshore fund listings and regular analytical statistical tables to the *WSJE* and then the Asian edition as well. We contacted Reuters seeking a similar but not identical deal, which we were never able to work out, but which years later led to the sale of the operating assets of my company to Reuters. In many ways I owed Phil and the Dow Jones senior management for one of the reasons that this book came to be: the cash wealth that was generated by my subsequent sale to Reuters. When Phil and his wife, Betsy, and their two daughters returned to the States, they moved into the town in which I live, Summit, New Jersey, a quite upscale town that has become something of a Wall Street and publishing ghetto. If I could help Phil with his new career, then I could repay the "due bill" that I felt I owed him.

The next hurdle was that I am not a natural writer. Like many analysts I believe minutiae are important, and this has led to Germanic sentences that go on forever. Phil suggested that I do this book with Doug Sease, a former writer and editor for the *WSJ*, where he produced columns of great depth but with few words. I had known Doug casually from his days at the *Journal*, but also from commuting, as he lived in Westfield, New Jersey, as I then did. Doug, since retiring from the *WSJ*, works on numerous book projects as well as enjoying his 46-foot sailboat in Florida. By early January 2007 the three of us had an agreement to produce this book. We have enjoyed working together largely through the Internet with few face-to-face meetings.

What kind of book did I want to write? For the last ten years, if not before, at the urging of my wife and soul mate Ruth, I have wanted to pass on to my four children the lessons that I have learned about the wealth that will pass through to them over their lifetimes. I have seen substantial wealth created and dissipated within my family and others. To put this into perspective, one has to know something about my family. I have already mentioned that in recent generations we have worked in Wall Street. Four different "Lipper" brokerage firms have been headed up by my grandfather, father, brother, and myself. Never has a younger brother or son taken over the leadership of one of these firms, and each firm eventually retired from the NYSE with our reputation and capital intact. While there were no direct transfers of ownership between the generations, some knowledge and perhaps instincts were passed on, as well as reputations, that allowed each Lipper to build on the network of prior firms.

With this kind of background one would think that I grew up with wealth, but that was not the case. My tuition to Columbia was paid for out of earnings from summer jobs and an NROTC scholarship, which led to a commission in the U.S. Marine Corps. What happened to the wealth that was generated from being connected to Wall Street for more than one hundred years? Now we come to one of the major reasons for this book. Money was dissipated through numerous divorces, nonworking members, and uncontrolled expenses. If all of life can be summed up in bank balances, one could be bitter about the forgone opportunities due to the failure to protect and build capital. I believe that this is much too narrow a view of life and wealth. To me wealth encompasses at least three elements: talent, networks, and financial capital. On these bases I come from a very wealthy family. In my generation, unlike me up to this point, we have a number of published authors, including my elder brother Arthur, who has written extensively on angel investing and other capital-intensive topics; Randa, a stepsister, on travel; Susan, my half sister, on fine-art photography; and my son Don, who with his wife has a business of freelancing articles for various publications. I also have a half brother who is a sportswriter with a regional newspaper.

Not only is there some printer's ink in the family, but also a glancing relationship with politics, mostly on the Republican side of the aisle. One of my mother's relatives wrote a book on how he was an elector, in the college of electors, for Abraham Lincoln. Another relative was one of the first female judges in the state of New York. My mother was a principal assistant to Wendell Willkie. My grandfather on my father's side used to enjoy telling the story of how he and Mark Hanna rode in a car together believing that they had sidestepped the nomination of Teddy Roosevelt for president by having him accept the vice-presidential nomination under the ill-fated William McKinley. Finally, my brother was appointed a page in the U.S. Senate by a respected Democratic senator from New York. Outside of testifying before Congress, my only other brush with the political world was via the former superintendent of my military school,

Major General Wilton B. Persons, who was recalled by General Eisenhower to serve as his second chief of staff in the White House after his first chief of staff left because of accepting gifts. Each of these contacts has been useful in helping me understand the interrelationship between international and domestic politics and investing in a practical way.

This generation of the family has contributed its time, efforts, and talents to numerous nonprofits and charitable organizations. We have been involved on both coasts with symphony orchestras and prestigious universities, among other activities. We have seen both the inside and outside of these organizations as volunteers, board members, and donors. These experiences have influenced my thinking on how to participate in these worthy organizations with our efforts and money. Sitting on numerous boards has given me insights on how others are dealing with their wealth of talent and capital.

When I began this project, I had four children: three sons and a daughter, who had learning difficulties all her life. For the last ten years my wife and I had worried what to do for Kay after we were no longer here. My three sons were given all the education that they could tolerate, as were their children. Kay was special in many ways, and Ruth, as her stepmother, helped her evolve into a lovely, caring adult. She was the principal focus of all our plans, from the house we lived in to special-needs trusts. On September 1, 2007, I was thrilled to walk her down the aisle for the wedding of her dreams. She, and it, were perfect thanks to Ruth. After a week's honeymoon she came back with a deep cough that she couldn't shake. Kay met Ruth at the emergency room at the good local hospital for a chest X-ray.

By three the next morning, she was admitted to the oncology ward at Overlook Hospital. She died on October 26 with stage 4 cancer, having been married for fifty-five days. Kay was the center of our life in many ways. We had never considered that she would leave this world before we did. We are rearranging our thinking for our estate and how we are going to take care of her husband. Her thoughts and desires will guide us, and thus Ruth and I are dedicating this book to Kay. During the difficult period of her hospitalization, death, and funeral, the need to finish the half-done book could have been questioned by many others. However, I remembered the second thing that one learns early in the Street and that I taught Kay: our word is our bond. Kay lived by this credo as well.

No book of life's lessons is ever the exclusive thought and experience of a single person. Without Phil's encouragement and the hard work by Doug of converting my overly complex thoughts and language, you would not be reading this book today. The assistance of my office ladies, led by Elaine Brady, was often required not only to transmit pieces to Doug but also to assist me in my other work and nonprofit responsibilities. The experience that Maureen Busby Oster has provided me in our work of accounts of wealthy families and institutions has proven invaluable. My co-managing member Zuheir Sofia has contributed his insights into the families of many of our financial-services hedge-fund investors. My three sons, Ken, Steve, and Don, contributed their strength to Ruth and me during this difficult time, in particular with their support of their new brother-in-law. All of their help both on the book and in putting our lives back together is a tribute to them and their love for their departed sister. Simply put, I could not have accomplished what I have over the last twenty-one years without my wife Ruth's support and counsel, which is in turn supported by her sisters and their families.

MONEY WISE

INTRODUCTION

Many people who do not have wealth believe that it bestows upon its holder a sense of well-being and satisfaction. Alas, they are often wrong and, were they to become wealthy, would soon discover why. Wealth brings with it tremendous responsibilities, not only to one's self and family, but to the general welfare of society. How wealth is generated, invested, and spent has a tremendous ripple effect through the economy and society. Some people handle the responsibilities of wealth well, and some handle them poorly. But the mere weight of the responsibility is often enough to create a vague sense of unease. Am I investing correctly? Can I trust my advisors? Are certain family members feeling slighted? How should I determine which worthy organizations will get part of my wealth?

Ridding oneself of these and other related concerns is not easy. I think I know why. Too many people are thinking too conventionally about every aspect of wealth. We all have heard the phrase *conventional wisdom,* something that "everybody knows" without knowing how or why we know it. In many cases the term should be a red flag indicating that the person using it is preparing to introduce some kind of "unconventional wisdom" that is intended to challenge the conventional wisdom. Beware! More often than not that unconventional wisdom is a thin disguise for a sales pitch for an unproven or unneeded product or service. Only occasionally does the unconventional wisdom really consist of a genuinely new way of thinking about a subject.

This is a book about selected unconventional ways of thinking about wealth. I am presenting my ideas here because I believe people of wealth can benefit from them. They are based on my personal experiences, those of my clients, and years of careful observation of the investment world as the founder of Lipper Analytical Services, the operating assets of which I sold in 1998. If my coauthor and I do our jobs well, you can use these ideas to think about and manage your wealth with increased satisfaction and greater confidence.

I emphasize that not all conventional wisdom is wrong. Quite the contrary. Most of it is right and should not be ignored in favor of ideas that are merely different. The problem with conventional wisdom is that it is too often stated in a summarization or a generalization that, while it might have broad applications, fails when applied to specific situations. That is particularly true in a financial environment, where no two situations are identical, yet broad generalizations are most often used as the foundation of decisions.

My objectives for the reader are threefold. First, to help

identify and think about what constitutes the conventional wisdom. Second, to understand the challenges confronting a person seeking satisfaction from wealth. Finally, to assist in the development of a series of philosophies and strategies that are tailored to individual needs.

I do not believe in complete solutions, and this book is certainly not an attempt to be a complete solution. I am not going to tell you that you should have 67 percent of your investment portfolio in equities, 32 percent in fixed income, and 1 percent in cash. Individuals and their circumstances are all different and are all constantly changing. Indeed, the one lesson that I hope comes through most clearly in this book is that one must at all times be prepared to recognize how change is affecting every aspect of your finances and life. People do not like change. We are comfortable with what is. But one cannot totally avoid change eventually. Little changes are happening to us all the time, and we manage them, for the most part, without even thinking about them. Even big changes, if they take place over time, can be handled with aplomb. Think about how different you are today from when you were an infant, a teenager, a young adult. Some of those life changes probably felt a little traumatic or confusing at the time, but now they are just memories, perhaps good, perhaps bad. But every so often there will be a monumental change, a life-altering event. Too few people are prepared to handle those changes, the ones most likely to disrupt one's sense of satisfaction and well-being.

Change in our own lives is one thing; change in our environment is quite another. Most people go through the various stages of maturation at about the same ages, thus at roughly the same pace. But scientific and technological change is occurring increasingly rapidly. As mankind left the nomadic stage, people probably traveled no more than a day from their home site during their entire life. A century ago most Americans did not travel more than one hundred miles from their homes during their lifetime. Today we routinely travel thousands of miles from our homes without thinking twice about it. A mere fifty years ago most business was transacted face-to-face. Today I have "virtual offices" with people in a number of locations whom I rarely see face-to-face, yet we communicate easily and frequently via the Internet. The pace of change has significant implications for investment portfolios. We know, based on history, that we can confidently predict that current forces at work in the world will lose some of their potency at some point. Precisely when is a more difficult question to answer. But the *most* difficult question to answer is what will replace them? This is one reason in this book I recommend investing in numerous possible new trends. I realize at the outset that my batting average will reflect more strikeouts than hits. That does not worry me. I am hoping that my production of runs will be reasonably high and that some of the successes will be huge. This approach lacks certainty, but anyone who is totally certain about something in the future is a fool or a liar.

The ideas I put forth here are arranged, I hope, logically, but are not intended to build on themselves sequentially. You can read the fifth chapter before the first and it should not make much difference. This book is for browsing. You can stop to read something of interest, skipping the topics that do not seem relevant. We have tried to keep the chapters short and to the point.

We are all overwhelmed with information; to be useful we need to explain our ideas as quickly and efficiently as possible. No one is likely to agree with everything written here, and that is fine. Mine is not the only correct approach. All I ask is that you question the assumptions that lead to disagreement. Thinking is what this book is really about.

—Mike Lipper
Summit, New Jersey

PART ONE

THE NATURE
OF WEALTH

1

PHYSICS AND INVESTING:
The Search for Eternal Truths

I have a deep interest in the creation, growth, and preservation of wealth. It has been the essence of my career. But lately I find that I also have a growing interest in a subject I struggled with in high school and college: physics. Partly that stems from my role as a trustee of the California Institute of Technology, home of the famed Jet Propulsion Laboratory and of thirty-one recipients of thirty-two Nobel Prizes. It is indeed a humbling experience to sit in a room full of people who understand deeply things that are beyond me. But I am also drawn to physics for another reason: just as physicists search for the eternal laws of the universe, I—and many others involved in finance—want to find the eternal truths of creating, growing, and preserving wealth. Using physics as an analogy for the universe of wealth helps me think about what is true, what is only perceived, and what one can and cannot do within known boundaries. This chapter is not a primer on physics, but a brief examination of how the laws of physics and investing often run parallel, and how this analogy guides my thinking.

Wealth is the result of our ability to deal with the abstract, to create value, to plan for the long term, to go against our instincts (for better or worse), and to link seemingly disparate phenomena. But if we approach wealth creation and investing in the same manner that physicists approach their discipline—with an open mind, performing many observations and doing some experiments to test hypotheses—we, too, can hope to identify some fundamental aspects that we can equate with the laws of physics.

One of the things you may remember about your physics class is that you did a lot of measuring, some of it precise. Measurement defined the results of experiments and accurately predicted the outcomes of various events. Like physics, finance is obsessed with measurement, sometimes seeking precision at the cost of accuracy. Let me illustrate what I mean by discussing for a moment the phenomenon we know as gravity, that force that keeps us all firmly grounded on Earth. Physicists understand the effects of gravity precisely, so much so that they can calculate exactly how to send a spacecraft to the moon and return it to Earth, or even to send a craft to circle other plants and moons. Yet physicists do not understand the gravitational phenomena known as black holes with any precision at all. What's inside a black hole? What happens to the matter drawn into it? They simply do not know. Despite that lack of precision, however, they do know that any description of the universe that does not take into account the presence of black holes is not accurate.

How does this apply to finance? The business of Lipper Analytical was to measure the performance of various fund-related offerings and rank them accordingly. With some financial instruments, notably money-market funds, performance among several will be very, very close to one another. To rank that performance accurately we sometimes had to carry out the calculations to many decimal places. But the difference in performance was so tiny that in practical terms it meant nothing to the investor seeking a money-market fund. Some other factor would almost certainly outweigh those tiny performance differences, such as that a given fund was part of the fund family the investor used for other reasons.

Six laws or observations from physics apply to investing. The first is that for every action there is an equal and opposite reaction. In my world of wealth management, this becomes the truism that for every dollar's worth purchased, a similar amount is sold. In the current dynamic global marketplace that means that a price is determined by the strength of the motivation of each side of a transaction. In a world of instantaneous distribution of news and information, one must assume that each party possesses the same or similar information, a principle that is at the heart of the efficient-market hypothesis, a subject I will shortly touch upon. Translated to popular language, this means you cannot presume that whoever is taking the other side of your trade is dumb or poorly informed. Indeed, you should consider the possibility that the other person may be smarter or better informed than you! For the most part, however, it is safe to presume knowledge is equal on both sides.

The second physical law is that a body in motion tends to stay in motion, and one at rest stays at rest. This concept explains the attraction to momentum investing, which is buying what is moving higher and selling securities that are declining. An important element of this law is the search for a catalyst to create movement, something that value investors particularly like to see, since that catalyst can often prompt others to see what the value investor sees. This causes prices and value to rise.

The third law of physics is that net force is equal to mass times acceleration. This law has particular value in looking at institutional investing. Markets do not move on the value of an idea. Markets move when a lot of capital is rapidly applied. This is often called the weight of money.

The fourth law is the law of gravity, which asserts that a ton of feathers will drop at the same speed as a ton of steel in a space without friction. This law suggests that within each rising price is the seed of its future decline.

Perhaps the biggest lesson from physics that applies to the financial world is leverage. In the physical world, leverage is created by a platform resting on a pivot point or fulcrum. Think of a seesaw at the playground. While most children go merrily up and down, one rascally kid always sends his playmate soaring into the air or crashing to the ground by the application of either too much force or too little.

Leverage in finance is the borrowing of funds to acquire or maintain ownership of an asset. The platform of this imaginary seesaw points in the direction of highest value. The initial weight represents the purchase price of the asset. At the other, "lower" end is the size of the borrowing. The pivot point or fulcrum represents the time of repayment. A simple example is making a 20 percent down payment for a home and borrowing—i.e., mortgaging—the remaining 80 percent. Assume the purchase price was $1 million, ignoring interest, maintenance, insurance, and real estate taxes (don't I wish!). If, eight years later, the selling price of the home is $2 million, the gain on a compounded basis would be 9 percent on the purchase price, which is not bad. But it would be 25 percent on the initial equity, which is far better than one can expect to realize from most other investments.

Now suppose the selling price is again $2 million, but the sale takes place after eighteen years instead of eight. In that case the rate of return on the original equity would be 4 percent. Finally, suppose that instead of rising, the price of the home drops. A 20 percent decline in the selling price from the original $1 million effectively wipes out the seller's equity. An even larger decline requires that the seller bring cash to the closing to clear his loan. A sale price of $700,000 for example, assuming the seller has made no payments on his mortgage beyond the interest due, would require a cash payment on closing of $100,000. All the lessons from the playground seesaw are present: unequal inputs and elapsed time, which can be simulated on the seesaw by merely moving the fulcrum closer to one end or the other of the plank. Leverage works well if the forces work as planned, but if the heavy weight that is suspending the lighter weight gets off at the bottom of the cycle, the lighter weight will fall. In the financial world, the problem is that the time of final transaction is uncertain and most often in the hands of the lender. The lender's moves can be dictated by declining prices and other conditions.

Still another attribute from physics aids our understanding of the financial world. If efficiency is described as the percent of input that is translated into output, the difference is labeled friction. In the financial world, commissions, market spreads, fees, operating expenses, and taxes are components of friction and should be considered in making transactions. Engineers try hard to produce efficient engines and other apparatus, but they never achieve 100 percent efficiency because of the embedded inefficiencies we find in the world, including wear and tear. The world of finance is the same.

Physics is an attempt to discover and describe reality. The hard part is that there is not a single reality. The physical reality that we all recognize—from the sun, the planets, and stars right down to boiling an egg for breakfast—is a very different place from the reality at the quantum level, where atoms may not be where we think they are and light consists of both waves and particles. Reality in the financial world differs, too. As an investor and a person of wealth you are part of the equation that determines your financial results, for better or worse. And because you and everyone you rely on for advice are all too human, you must recognize that differing emotions, biases, and motivations will create alternative realities that have an effect on your outcomes. As humans we seek to understand the world around us and to influence it to act in our favor. We want things to be simple enough that we can think we understand them, and we often go out of our way to avoid pain at the cost of gain. As a result we often seek and use what is commonly known as conventional wisdom. But conventional wisdom frequently creates in our minds too simple a view of how the world works and, as a result, assigns greater importance to many events than they deserve. The more fundamental laws we can discover and use to correct our all-too-human tendencies, the better our results will be. So let us move now from the esoteric world of physics to the more down-to-earth realm of conventional wisdom and the problems associated with it.

2

THE SKEPTICAL INVESTOR:
What's Wrong with Conventional Wisdom?

I explained in the introduction that this is a book that offers unconventional thinking about the creation, preservation, and use of wealth. But what, you are almost certainly asking, is wrong with conventional wisdom? Let me begin with a few succinct statements about conventional wisdom to set the stage for a more thorough discussion about why I think unconventional wisdom is important.

Conventional wisdom is what most people talk about and some believe.

Conventional wisdom is something people think they know without knowing how or why they know it.

Conventional wisdom is accepted as being true because it is not challenged.

Conventional wisdom can be delivered in sound bites.

Conventional wisdom is based on the extrapolation of near-term results.

Implicit or explicit in every statement of conventional wisdom is the phrase *all other things being equal.*

None of those statements, you will notice, says anything about whether conventional wisdom is right, although I should note that all other things are *never* equal. Conventional wisdom can often be correct, but my professional life has been that of an analyst, and a good analyst is, at heart, a skeptic. My job over the years has been to think unthinkable thoughts and to question everything. When you apply that approach to statements of conventional wisdom about the creation, preservation, and use of wealth, you often find that even if it is not wrong, conventional wisdom is not useful. The flaws in conventional wisdom are myriad. Too often conventional wisdom ignores complexity, has not been tested and proven, is based on assumptions that are unwarranted, or does not take into account individual circumstances. In short, conventional wisdom is *too simple.*

Do not misunderstand. Simple is not bad. Indeed, some of the most important insights into nature and the human mind can be stated simply. Take the famous equation $E = mc^2$. It does not get much simpler than that: three letters, a number, and a mathematical symbol. Yet that simple formula is the most profound description of the universe as we know it that has ever been devised. It literally changed history. And while, as I said in the previous chapter, I know relatively little about physics, I know that the simple equation that Einstein devised is the result of a prodigious amount of thinking, testing, and analyzing

17

that stretches back for centuries. Yes, $E = mc^2$ is simple, but it captures and distills amazing complexity. And that is where conventional wisdom too often fails: it is not the result of the distillation of complexity through thought and analysis. It is meant to apply to everybody at every time. Yet without rigorous testing we cannot assume that conventional wisdom, even if true for the moment, will be fully true at all times. Further, I believe that you, as an individual decision maker, affect your own results to an extent that conventional wisdom, while right at the moment for others, may not be right for you.

This is not to say that we cannot use conventional wisdom to our advantage. We just have to understand that conventional wisdom is always based on certain assumptions. Heeding conventional wisdom without knowing and understanding the assumptions behind it increases the risk that the conventional wisdom is not true in a specific case. We need to know the conditions under which the assumptions will correctly work to be able to take advantage of conventional wisdom or to know when to ignore it.

Take, for example, the popular notion that the return from stocks in the long run beats the return from bonds. This is based on the assumption that stocks will benefit from the long-term secular growth of the economy while the returns on bonds are fixed (that is why bonds are called fixed income). But here the unsophisticated investor tends to fall prey to the fallacy of averages. Yes, on average, stock averages usually outperform bonds over the long run (depending on what you assume "the long run" is). But not every stock outperforms, and, in fact, there is no such thing as the "average stock." Each is different and each contains its own risks. For many years AT&T was a "safe" stock. That changed instantly when Judge Harold Greene ordered the company broken up in 1982, and investors who held AT&T because they assumed it was safe had their convictions painfully shaken. Applying the conventional wisdom about stocks on average to a specific stock can lead to disaster. Remember, American Cotton Oil was once one of the stocks in the Dow Jones Industrial Average (only General Electric among the original stocks still exists as a company, and today's GE very definitely isn't your father's GE!).

Let me take a few paragraphs to illustrate how conventional wisdom applied to investing can be mistaken or, at the very least, not useful. We can start with the seemingly intelligent approach to investing that commands us to invest in well-managed companies and avoid poorly managed companies. It sounds logical enough, yet we have consistently made money in companies that were not well managed at the time and have not been able to equal that performance by investing in well-managed companies. The difference is that the stock prices of well-managed companies reflect that good management, while the prices of the poorly managed companies reflect the burden of their poor management. If the management of the poorly managed companies changes for the better, the stock price rises to reflect that change. Since management at the well-managed company can only change for the worse, the risk that the stock price will fall rather than rise, at least based on perceptions of management, is fairly large.

That leads us to a discussion of the conventional wisdom embodied in the efficient-market theorem devised by my friend

Professor Burton Malkiel, to whom my old firm supplied data over the years. The theorem tells us that everything known about a security is captured in its price. But market dynamics can, at least in the short range, disrupt prices abnormally. For example, if I want to buy a million shares of a stock, I have to consider what happens to the price of that stock under at least two different approaches to making the purchase. What if, for example, I suddenly enter an order for a million shares? That order will instantly attract the attention of professional traders, who will understand that the demand for the stock has suddenly improved. They will use their resources to buy that stock for their own accounts, either to sell to me as my huge trade works its way through the system, or on the speculation that so much demand will spur even more demand. The price of the stock skyrockets. Then, when my order has been filled and everyone realizes that I was the only one demanding the stock, all those traders will realize their mistake and bail out of their positions, sending the price into a steep plunge.

But what if instead of placing a single sudden order I parcel my purchases out over two months, buying twenty thousand shares here, ten thousand there on a given day, then sitting on the sidelines for a few days doing nothing? Some traders, notably the specialists in the stock, will catch on that something is going on with the stock and may begin buying it, too, on the assumption that whatever is going on will net them a profit. But the stock price will almost certainly not rise to the extent it would have under my single million-share buy order, nor will it fall nearly as far when it becomes clear that I am an isolated buyer. In the end, I own the same million shares in either case, but the price performance, my costs, and the impact on the market is quite different in each scenario.

Circumstances can easily refute many other tidbits of conventional wisdom. Peter Lynch gained his fabulous reputation as a stock picker at least in part by telling stories about how he stumbled across great stock picks by discovering a product he loved and buying stock in the company that made it. Yet plenty of companies with great products did not have the management to make a profit from the products and went out of business. Another maxim is to avoid buying shares of a company that has a complex organizational structure. Yet I find that if I take the time and effort to deconstruct that complex organization and understand it, I have an advantage over a competitor who thinks it is simply too much trouble to analyze.

While I have spent my life studying the way markets work and can frequently determine if the assumptions underlying some piece of conventional wisdom are appropriate to the situation, most of you reading this do not have that background. You can do it in your own field of expertise, but I recommend that you consult a professional with a historical viewpoint of the markets to help you understand and interpret conventional wisdom as it applies to your wealth and investments. (I'll talk more about this later.) And even then, because markets are creations of the human mind and not physical laws of the universe, you can still get it wrong.

The point of this discussion about conventional wisdom is twofold. First, I want you to understand my perspective as an advisor to people of wealth and as an investor in my own right. Knowing how I view the world will inform your further reading of the chapters, whether you read them sequentially or just pick topics that interest you. Second, I want you to come away from this discussion with a new level of skepticism about all you hear about wealth management and investing. In fact, I want you to apply that skepticism to this book. Do not take what I say here at face value. Question it, especially as you perceive it applies to you. Use what you find useful, discard what you do not. If nothing else, I want you to think at least a little bit differently about your wealth than you did before and differently from all those around you. Wealth is an individual phenomenon, and your approach to it should reflect your individuality.

3

A SIMPLE QUESTION:
Why Do We Invest?

F ew of the hundreds and hundreds of investment-advice books delve into the most basic question of all: why do we invest? It's a simple question, but it doesn't have a simple answer. Indeed, it has at least five different answers, one or some of which are applicable to virtually any investor. Yet few new-account application forms or even initial interviews with money managers dig deeply enough to get at those answers.

The first answer is that we believe that we have been given or have earned assets, including our intangible assets of health, energy, intelligence, and the sense that we are here for a reason beyond mere existence. This belief impels us to control our assets for reasons beyond self-aggrandizement. We want to safeguard the assets and, if possible, grow their value. In effect, we become the stewards of our assets. As such, most of us who have accumulated substantial assets know inherently that protecting those assets—*putting them under the mattress* is the oft-used expression—isn't the answer. Instead we follow the biblical injunction that teaches us as stewards to both protect and invest our assets wisely.

The second answer stems from our belief that inflation, which is, in effect, a devaluation of our currency, is a normal condition of the economy. The only question is how severe the inflationary trend will be over time. But whether inflation is severe or mild, holding assets without investing them results in declines in the purchasing power of those assets. The greatest loss that stems from any major market decline is paid by those so rattled by the drop in market values that they refuse to invest again once the crisis has passed. They not only suffer the tangible losses resulting from the market declines, but they also pay a much stiffer price in terms of opportunity costs, those losses being greatest in times when inflation is greatest. And while inflation has been tame in recent years, never forget that the United States has in memory endured low-double-digit inflation, and emerging markets have encountered truly savage triple-digit inflation.

The third answer lies in our need to grow our asset base and/or related income to meet selected goals. We attempt to eliminate the difference between the value of our assets today and the specific defined needs of the future. In many ways this answer poses the biggest problems to us as investors simply because we must often guess what our specific needs will be in the future, within a reasonable range, before determining the approaches that will enable us to close the gap between that estimate and the assets we hold today.

The fourth answer revolves around our very human instinct to compete. Many of the wealthiest people in the financial world, if not elsewhere, have more money than they can possibly require in a lifetime. They have long ago satisfied their earthly needs and those of their loved ones. Yet they have a profound need to have, or at least be thought to have, more money than the next millionaire, deca-millionaire, centi-millionaire, or just simply billionaire. They crave the thrill of the game and money is how they keep score. Some of these "players" wind up as adrenaline junkies who desperately need to take a shot of risk regularly.

Finally, some people invest so they can sound knowledgeable at various dinners or cocktail parties. In some circles the market is one of the first topics of conversation, often followed by real estate, taxes, politics, and allusions to sex. Of these, "smart" comments about the market are the safest opening gambits at the beginning of a long evening.

After determining the answer, or in many cases how you rank the priority of the two or more answers, you can start to build a portfolio that at least addresses your real needs as an investor. Investing for or with a steward requires a high level of certainty that in a reasonable time there will be no significant losses to the account's overall value despite the ability to tolerate losses in individual holdings. Most stewards, fearing that they can be called to account at any time both for the maintenance and the growth of the assets, have a great compulsion to invest only in the highest-quality bonds, stocks, and funds among other assets. We would typically use only U.S. Treasuries of short, rolling maturities for the maintenance requirement and stocks or funds of the highest quality. The result will be dull but comfortable.

Investors who are conscious of inflation also wish to avoid losses, but in this case they see the biggest potential loss is not the cyclical movements of stocks but the steady erosion of value by inflation. The appropriate portfolio for this kind of investor would only hold money-market funds and funds consisting of Treasury Inflation Protected Securities (TIPS), which adjust for the government's announced inflation rates. The stock side of the portfolio would have two elements. The first is invested in securities related to currently scarce commodities. The trick here is to know when to get out of a particular commodity and/or all commodities. Only a few managers or advisors have a track record of leaving the game near the peak of popularity. The second and usually much larger part of the equity portfolio is investments in companies whose unit-sales growth is expected to be larger than the average expected inflation.

The investor looking to fill the gap between today's asset values and future needs probably owns little or no fixed-income securities and invests in equities or stock funds that have been successful over the years at producing sustainable growth. For the last thirty-five years the surviving diversified equity funds have produced an average annual return of 10.5 percent, which includes some loss years and some with gains of over 20 percent. While no one can predict the long term, for planning purposes over at least a generation, returns slightly in excess of 10 percent seem reasonable today. In this area, funds ranked highly on the consistency of their returns should be examined for inclusion in a portfolio.

The competitive investor often looks for extreme investments. Too many look at the current "tops of the pops" or leading funds or managers. This can work for some temperamentally suited investors who jump out as quickly as they jump in regardless of tax implications. Many of the better managers and funds don't want this kind of investor and, when possible, refuse their money. In a world that supplies a product for any well-funded need, a number of open-ended funds, often using leverage, invest in a predetermined portfolio that is available for those who believe they have market-timing skills. For those who prefer not to be invested in leveraged portfolios, over four hundred Exchange Traded Funds, or ETFs, are available. The fund analyst in me suggests that another way for competitive investors to find their "fix" is to look for funds that have had poor absolute performance for one or more years within a reasonably good long-term relative performance. When these funds start to have good short-term performance in terms of weeks, not months, the momentum tides could be turning in their favor. At this point there is probably relatively little market risk because few believers are left. If whatever is driving the short-term momentum is soundly based, one could be looking at the next quarter's leader.

The investor who needs to be entertained or to be entertaining should focus on already well-known managers or funds that use the media as a marketing tool. Daily, but certainly weekly, visits to their Web sites or a Web search for their names will reveal their relative popularity and keep you abreast of their latest news and views. Follow your manager as if he or she were a sports star. That way you become something of an investment celebrity watcher.

Since most of us have multiple reasons for investing, you can use these various approaches in some combination. However, I would suggest that you keep your portfolio segregated by needs or, better yet, have separate portfolios so that you can track their respective results and be sure that you are dividing your assets in the proper order of your priorities.

4

THE WEALTH FORMULA:
A(ssets) = F(reedom)

M any wealthy people were once not so wealthy. Then they often had more "needs" (including debts to others) than they had money, or assets. Most people in that situation tend to think of having more assets as equivalent to having more freedom. To put in semi-mathematical terms, A(ssets) = F(reedom). But when people think of the equation A = F, they somehow tend to overlook the = sign. They forget that, mathematically speaking, both sides of an equation have to balance. What that means is that the more we have, the more is expected of us by government, family, friends, charities, and salespeople of every type.

If equations always balance, how do we obtain the freedom we want?

The answer is simple: change the equation!

Millionaires who stay millionaires can control their spending. That is not always easy. After all, any fool can spend all that he or she has or will ever get. So we will modify the equation a bit to make it a more complete picture of how things work:

$$A(ssets) - L(iabilities) + I(ncome) - S(pending) = E(xcess) \ A(ssets)$$

The key to how this equation affects our lives is that *excess assets are the basis for all investing.* And excess assets should not be measured in numbers alone. Included in the concept is a comfort level, that is, the possession of a sufficient quantity of assets to provide psychological security, at least in terms of wealth. Too many people measure their assets by comparing them to what they think others possess rather than more correctly looking at absolute levels of wealth. A case in point is an extremely wealthy woman from Florida who visited California during the dot-com heyday. What she saw shocked her. The dot-com millionaires were rolling in money and spending it as fast as they made it. Conspicuous consumption was rampant. Her exposure to all that new money destroyed her comfort level with her own wealth. Her asset base had not declined at all. She was, by any reasonable measure, still quite wealthy. But her psychological unwillingness to spend her money was destroyed by the conspicuous spending she observed in California. To regain her comfort level she instructed that her assets be redeployed to produce more income and realized gains, that is, a larger income stream that she could then spend without guilt. As we know, there are always trade-offs in investing. To obtain those higher returns her assets had to be redirected toward more speculative investments. Soon her income had increased and she felt her spending habits were on par with those of the dot-com million-aires. Unfortunately, she was also on the same risk level as they were. When the dot-com bubble predictably ended badly in 2000, her speculative investments suffered a major blow. The decline was not as severe as that which many of the dot-commers suffered—many lost virtually everything—and unlike them she could use her remaining assets to return to a comfortable spend-ing rate and lifestyle. What we learn from that woman's experi-ence is that the rate of spending not only sets the size of the available investment pool, but how it is going to be invested. This tale also demonstrates that excess assets do give one more free-dom to either spend or invest. The point is, if you want to create or preserve excess assets, don't rely on investing to do it. Investing re-turns are variable and not always positive, and you have little con-trol over variability. You do, however, have substantial control over your spending.

Now let us move on to another, simpler equation:

$$E(xcess)\ A(ssets) = M(ore)\ F(reedom)$$

The good news in that formula is that excess assets give you more freedom to choose where and how to invest. The bad news is that excess assets also become an incentive for others who want to make money by serving as your agent or intermediary. There are many ways to distinguish between kinds of investment advisors, but the simplest is to break them into two categories: those who are paid for their time and those who are paid out of the use and disposition of your assets. As an investor you can im-pose strict limits on how much the first category is rewarded by simply spending less time seeking their advice. The second group, however, has a substantial incentive to use various techniques, such as operating or financial leverage, to increase your assets and thus the share of those assets that they earn. Those techniques often expose a pool of assets to a level of risk not well understood by the client. The advisors in this second group tend to be good salespeople as well as your "new best friend." Make no mistake, some are good investors, but it is difficult to separate the wheat from the chaff in this category. While the government has imposed some disclosure regulations on advisors who deal with the general public, those regulations are often not imposed on those who work with the wealthy. The government, wrongly to my view, equates wealth with sophistication. A person with annual income in excess of $200,000 and/or assets in excess of $1 million (not including a principal residence) is deemed by the government to be a sophisticated investor and can thus be offered investments that are not allowed to be offered to the general investing public. One purpose of this book is to aid you in recognizing your own level of investment sophistication, which I believe has little or nothing to do with the relative size of your income or assets, but is related to your "wealth" of business and investment experience. Most investment cookbooks focus on the various investment instruments that are available or a single investment philosophy. I firmly believe that a person of wealth needs to think in more primitive, almost Darwinian, terms: it's YOU VS. THE WORLD.

Most people come out of the womb fighting to survive and continue that fight every day until the day they invariably lose the battle. This primordial drive, the need to survive, is reflected to some degree in our desire for investment survival. I won't go so far as to call it a "need" for investment survival, but the "desire" for investment survival. The difference in intensity between these two drives will have more to do with your success in each than will your choice of instruments or intermediaries. Your investments and the results they achieve are a function not only of how much money you bring to the process, but also many other factors, including effort, energy, intellect, integrity, and willingness to recognize what you do not know. The results will also be affected by your experience in judging people, by your ability to form and use social networks, and by your awareness of what is going on around you, not just in business and finance, but also in politics, religion, science, technology, and even the arts. And because each of us is different in the amount of time, effort, and ability we bring to the party, our results will be unique.

SOURCES OF WEALTH ARE DIFFERENT
FROM INVESTMENT USES OF WEALTH

Money has to come from somewhere. Both where it comes from and when it arrives have tremendous impact on our investment decisions. To understand our money and how we are going to be comfortable about spending it, we need to place ourselves in a framework that tells us something about ourselves and our relationship to wealth. I think in terms of three types of investors depending upon the source of their wealth.

New money: These are self-made millionaires. They certainly have no desire to return to the period before they made their fortunes, but their youthful outlook (which has nothing to do with chronological age) leads them to believe they could start all over and do it again if they had to. They have fond memories of the narcotic-like rush of taking high risks in the quest for big gains. Should they sell their business, they may feel as if they are only borrowing the proceeds from that business as capital, along with their now certain confidence that they can do it again, to start up another enterprise or take over an existing business to save it or grow it more rapidly.

Old money: These are the wealthy people who are two or more generations away from the "working stiffs" who created the family fortune. They live in terror that they may lose it all because they have no confidence that they could start over and re-create their fortunes.

Creating money: These people inhabit the middle ground between new money and old money. They are executives, particularly of large, successful companies. While they may have diversified their portfolios to some degree, the bulk of their wealth is tied up in their company's stock. They share some of the characteristics of the young-in-spirit entrepreneur as well as the trust-fund recipient, but approach investing differently. Like the entrepreneur they have specific knowledge and a developed network of people confined mostly to a single sector. They have some doubts that they could rebuild their wealth if a significant portion disappeared. Often as senior-level retirees they have substantial continuing pension payments for themselves and possibly their spouses that are analogous to the trust-fund payments received by the inherited-wealth group.

A key question for all three types of wealthy investors is whether the wealth is yours to do with as you please or are you acting as a steward of that wealth with the intention of sharing it with family and charities during your lifetime or later? Your answer to this question, coupled with the type of investor you are, has a tremendous influence on your spending rate as well as on the investment time horizon you establish. (Be very wary of thinking in perpetual terms.)

A final question: whom do you expect to talk to and get advice from about investments? It may be a small "kitchen cabinet" of informal advisors, including your spouse, children, good friends, accountant, lawyers, or trust officer. If these are conventional thinkers, their advice may limit your investment horizons. Another group might be your network of associates, colleagues, and business friends. You will be surprised at how many people you know directly and, in turn, how many people to whom they can introduce you. This network can be a critical source of advice for someone who is attempting to preserve wealth because they have had direct contact with senior managers or know people who know the senior managers of companies you might want to add to your investment portfolio. One rule that I try to follow is not to make a serious investment if I cannot find someone who has been in the same room with the principals of the company under consideration and seen them under some pressure. I am constantly amazed at how many second or third degrees of separation exist through which I can find helpful contacts or insights. I have known many people of importance both in the investment world and the regulatory world on a first-name basis because we were analysts together or my work with mutual funds brought me to their attention. Knowing how they acted in the past has given me a good indication how they would act presently or in the future under somewhat similar circumstances.

5

BALANCING YOUR BOOKS:

The Art of Matching Assets and Liabilities

L ike me, you've probably been called many things in your life, but I bet this is the first time you've been called a balance sheet. In financial terms, you are a living, breathing combination of assets and liabilities. Knowing the balance between those assets and liabilities is a crucial part of setting your priorities and reaching your goals. But it is not as easy as you think.

In your dealings with financial institutions you've probably compiled one or more "statements of net worth." Those statements purport to be the net results of combining your assets and your liabilities, and the numbers are probably pretty "hard" since you obtain many of them from bank statements or brokerage records. But those statements of net worth, while useful to the financial institutions, are only marginally useful for you. They do not get at the heart of your personal balance sheet.

The balance sheet I have in mind will, like your earlier statements of net worth, be a summary of various numbers classified
as either assets or liabilities. Some of these numbers will of ne-
cessity be "soft," basically nothing more than your educated
guess. Do not worry about that right now. You should be reviewing and revising your personal balance sheet at least annually,
and with each iteration you'll get a better feel for values. The
point of the balance sheet exercise is twofold. First, it is not so
much to set out specific numbers as it is to make guesses about
the ultimate size of your assets and liabilities. Second, you will
use it to build your own philosophy of wealth and to assign specific assets to specific goals. Wealthy people lead complex lives,
with many demands, obligations, goals, and means. Everyone's
life is different, and you are the driver of your own set of com-
plexities. Your personal balance sheet becomes a source of
knowledge that you can use to solve your personal series of
simultaneous equations. If you and your spouse or companion
commingle your assets, you can do a single balance sheet. If you
do not, you should each prepare your own.

Assets first. Start with your residence. You almost certainly
count that among your assets, and it's probably right up there
among the top four or five on your statement of net worth. But
the value you assigned it on that statement—your approximation
of what you could sell it for given recent sales of similar
properties—is only valid for your personal balance sheet if you're
carried out of the house dead or decide that your fondest ambition is to move in with your kids. Otherwise, the value of your
house is substantially less than what it would sell for simply because you would have to replace it with another place to live.

Assume for a moment that you and your spouse do really intend to be carried dead out of your house. Its value on your personal balance sheet under that circumstance is zero since you will not realize any gain on it. Instead, it becomes an asset in your estate plan, that is, an asset on someone else's personal balance sheet (more about heirs later). You may, of course, plan to sell your house before you die, but then you're faced with where to live. You may replace it by purchasing another house, either more or less expensive, or you may decide to rent a place instead of buying it. Whatever the case, your estimate of your home's value on your personal balance sheet has to reflect the reality that you cannot, while alive, realize the entire value that you would get for it in a sale. There's one caveat here: your house, if paid for, affords you substantial borrowing power that can serve as a "contingent asset"—you do not use it unless you need it—to offset an unanticipated need.

If you're still working, the next item on the asset side of your personal balance sheet is your career. I know, you did not list that on your statement of net worth for the mortgage company. Nevertheless it is a significant asset that represents not just near-term money, but also the possibility of substantial deferred income. For many of us our career is a shorthand way of describing our knowledge base. Our career is what we know how to do well. While our knowledge base usually extends far beyond the confines of our career, it is usually impossible to quantify much of that knowledge. Your career, however, has its own somewhat quantifiable value, and beyond that, your career also drives other costs that directly influence your balance sheet, such as where you live, how you entertain, and where and how often you travel.

Unfortunately, for most of us, particularly those over age fifty, it becomes increasingly unlikely that we could replace our current job with one that provides as much or more income and long-term value. Even if you own your business, there's no guarantee that it will survive over the long term amid today's vicious local and global competition. In this first pass at compiling a personal balance sheet, assign your job a value equal to a year's pay, including bonuses, plus the after-tax value of unexercised options if you have them.

You may also be in line to inherit substantial assets eventually. Money is a touchy subject in many families, and you may not know the precise amount destined to pass to you or how it is currently invested, only that it could be substantial. Nevertheless, make a stab at estimating the amount because it could be an important part of your financial future assuming the person bequeathing the money does not change his or her mind or live much longer than you expect. Your estimation should be based on a set of assumptions about things you know for a fact: you have two brothers, so assume your parent's estate will be divided three ways, unless you know your parents intend to divvy up the estate based on each child's needs.

These three items—your house, career, and inheritance—are intended to show you how to think about the value of various assets that are difficult to price. These elements are by no means an exhaustive list. You will almost certainly find other categories of "soft" assets in your life. One of the softest yet most valuable assets you have is your network of contacts. While impossible to quantify, for most of us this asset grows in depth and value for much of our lives.

Once you've compiled your list of soft assets, you can add to the list the standard hard numbers, such as balances in bank accounts, securities accounts, bonds, second homes, and other assets that are easily quantifiable and reasonably liquid.

Now we turn to the liability side of the ledger. In your earlier statements of net worth you may well have listed no liabilities. You may not have a mortgage, a car loan, or a current credit-card balance. But that does not mean your personal balance sheet has no liabilities, some of which you may currently think of not so much as liabilities but as "goals." Do you intend to fund educational expenses for your children or grandchildren? Is your health going to be perfect until you suddenly drop dead? Do you intend to travel, eat in fine restaurants, and engage in other lifestyle indulgences after you retire? They're all liabilities on your personal balance sheet, and many of them are, like some of your assets, difficult to estimate. Yet it is important that you make the effort because your estimate of your liabilities drives the way in which you arrange your assets.

You may not think of it as a liability, but the routine cost of living—and the increase in that cost over time—is going to be your biggest long-term obligation and the most important in terms of proper funding. Unless you are particularly profligate, if you are still working, you are almost certainly covering your living expenses easily with plenty left over. Once your employment income ends, however, those same expenses can quickly become a drain. I know most people talk about cutting back on expenses when they retire, but they seldom make significant reductions. Thus you need to do some serious investigation of your spending habits now so that you can estimate the total liability they represent. Since few of us know how long we will live, I suggest projecting living expenses out to at least age eighty-five and including at least a 3 percent annual inflation rate.

One of the most fearsome liabilities you may face is health care for you and your spouse and perhaps other family members. Insurance and Medicare will almost certainly cover a portion of your health-care costs from now until your death, but they will almost equally certainly not cover them all. Much hinges on the nature of the decline in your health, your willingness to spend for specialists and drugs, and how it all affects your lifestyle. A first stab at estimating health-care costs might be to find out the daily rate for a private room in the hospital that would be your first choice in the event of a major illness. If you're in good health now, multiply that daily rate by something between 30 and 90, depending on your age and health, to derive a liability number. If you have a serious chronic disease, such as diabetes, multiply by 90 to 180. Some serious, progressive problems, such as Parkinson's, might warrant multiplying by 360 or more. The resulting number may be shockingly high, but keep in mind that we're using the hospital daily rate as a proxy for even-more-difficult-to-estimate costs of specialists and pharmaceuticals.

Education for your children or grandchildren may be another big liability. Most people are most concerned about paying for college educations, but I think you get the most bang for the buck by funding attendance at a top-rated secondary or high school. The next most effective "investment" in a child's education is an excellent primary school. Estimates of the cost of college educations should reflect your judgment of each child's ability. An ambitious child with good grades and an aptitude for learning suggests budgeting for four years of tuition, room, and board at a top university. Fallback positions, again depending upon aptitude and ambition, would be second-tier private colleges, top-tier state universities, and so on to various occupational schools. Postgraduate education poses its own problems in the "bang for the buck" department. Law, medical, and business degrees usually reap big financial returns for the student. Advanced degrees in English and the arts are not as remunerative. If your child really wants an advanced degree in poetry, consider that you might want to use the assets that would pay for the degree to instead set up a trust to help pay the cost of living until the child is economically independent.

Your estate—what you want to leave to heirs—is yet another liability. Again, choosing a number is not easy. Some people dismiss it with a flip comment such as "Whatever is left is what they get." If you are one of those and seriously mean it, then you have no estate liability. Everyone else should, though, make an effort to come up with a number (here's where your house value enters the picture) and to allocate that amount by the number of heirs and the amounts you wish to direct to them.

When you finish this exercise, you'll have a clearer picture of the way in which you need to allocate your wealth to achieve your goals. Each specific liability should have some specific assets dedicated to it. Which assets are directed toward which goals depends on the time horizon to meet the goal. A college education fund for a sixteen-year-old National Merit Finalist has to be fully funded now with conservatively invested and reasonably liquid assets. The college education fund for a six-year-old first-grader can be partially funded now and invested in riskier assets with higher potential returns while you direct another batch of assets toward the imminent expense of a private primary school. Some goals can be met out of cash flow—annual charitable contributions, for example—while others, such as a sizable bequest to your alma mater, may be part of your estate and funded through a mix of assets, including a part of the value of your house.

Your personal balance sheet is a living document. It should be brought up-to-date at least annually, perhaps on your birthday or when you are gathering information to prepare your income tax return for the previous year, to reflect your changing circumstances and those of the world around you. If you are reasonably conservative in funding and investing for your various liabilities and goals, you will probably have an excess of assets matched against any single goal. Then, as certain goals are met—that National Merit Finalist graduates from Caltech—the excess assets can be redeployed somewhere else. Given the complexity of most people's lives, numerous assets will be invested in various ways for different lengths of time. The beauty of this approach is that you can concentrate the assets allocated to any particular liability in the single most appropriate investment to generate optimum returns, yet your overall portfolio will be well diversified and thus protected from the unexpected shocks that occasionally disrupt markets and economies.

6

FEAR AND GREED:
Growing Your Balance Sheet

Now that you have a new and expanded notion of your net worth, you will almost certainly want to grow your balance sheet. Few among us really want to take the risk that is inherent in trying to spend our last dollar on our last day. Instead you will want to at least keep pace with, if not stay well ahead of, increasing liabilities and spending. And it is not just liabilities and spending in the present that will increase. Your "completion spending"—my euphemism for the distribution of your assets after death—will likely continue to rise, too. Hopefully, you will not be entering the completion-spending phase anytime soon, but like taxes, death is inevitable.

Why will your liabilities, spending, and completion expenses continue to rise over time? The answer encompasses two certainties and one probability. The first certainty is inflation. Inflation has been relatively tame for a number of years, but even tame inflation takes a toll over time. A mere 3 percent annual inflation rate would wipe out non-income-producing accounts in twenty-four years and a 6 percent rate would destroy them in just twelve years. There is no guarantee that price increases will not accelerate, perhaps seriously, in coming years. The uncertain supply-and-demand equation for energy alone is worrisome. The second certainty is that our enormously creative and powerful economy will continue to turn out innovative new products and services as well as make enormous improvements in existing products—think of information technology, pharmaceuticals, and entertainment, for example—that will command an increasing share of your wallet. The probability is involvement. One of the insidious ways both your presumed family heirs as well as various nonprofits try to improve or perhaps guarantee their rank order among those destined to receive your "goodies" is to get you to invest more time with them now. The more time you invest with them, they hope, the greater will be your allocation to them in your completion-spending phase. I have observed that the technique is often effective.

One might argue that at some point "enough is enough" and the desire to continue growing assets becomes pure greed. Indeed, in the pop psychology of financial salesmanship, the only two drivers behind financial decisions are fear and greed. That's a vast oversimplification, but it can be a useful way of thinking about our financial lives. What may surprise you, however, is that I have found that it is almost always a complex amalgam of fears, not greed, that drives even the wealthiest to make decisions about growing their assets. There are many definitions of greed, but a useful one is the strong desire to accumulate assets far in excess of one's needs. For those who truly are greedy, the solution is simple: get more. It is much more difficult to grapple with fear. People do not wish to be afraid, and one of the drives to be wealthy is to escape fear. Nevertheless the fear of disappointing yourself or your beneficiaries in innumerable ways lies behind many of the decisions that the wealthy make about using their wealth. While for the greedy there may never be enough, one aim of this book is to help you quell the various fears with a well-reasoned and defined analysis of your financial and investment philosophy.

You can determine whether your primary motivator is fear or greed by remembering the last several financial conversations you had at social events. Often someone in the group is boasting about some investment success, albeit without disclosing how his or her overall account is performing. You might guess that the boastful speaker is being driven by greed. But if you hear the same boast more than once, you can be fairly certain that the person is acting out of fear, in this case the fear that unless he contributes his story to the conversation, his peers might think he has nothing to say and conclude he is, shall we say, on the dim side? He is forgetting that old adage that if you keep your mouth shut, people can only guess whether you're dumb; once you open it, they know for sure.

Contrast that kind of conversation with the many I have had over the years with some of the best money managers, legends in their own right. For the most part the conversation focuses not on their triumphs, but on their periods of relatively poor performance or the opportunities they missed. To some degree they are like the fisherman who talks for hours about "the big one that got away." These investment geniuses are not exhibiting false humility or being humble. Instead, they are using the give-and-take of conversation to search for clues to avoid repeating their mistakes and to discern possible areas of future interest to investigate. These are the greedy ones, striving for continued long-term gains in a game in which money is the measure of who is winning and who is losing. They are echoing the Goldman Sachs marketing theme that the firm is "long-term greedy."

Fear as a motivator can be corralled and brought under control through two very different concepts that are, in the end, closely related. The first is fiduciary duty. Think of yourself as a fiduciary, one to whom property or power is entrusted for the benefit of another and who stands in a special relationship of trust, confidence, and responsibility to the other.

You may be a formal fiduciary, such as a trustee or director who can, under law, be penalized for misdeeds, but not for poor judgments. More likely, your role as a fiduciary is informal, nothing more than the feeling that you have a responsibility to others to watch over and manage assets that are theirs or will one day be. Formal or informal fiduciary, you do not want to disappoint them. Further, you do not want to be embarrassed by being lax about your responsibilities or by making a major irreversible mistake. The key to serving as a fiduciary is to be certain that money is sufficient now and in the long term to meet the challenges of inflation and taxes and still accomplish the various missions.

The second concept, one that is an important function of a fiduciary, is controlled spending. Formal fiduciaries of nonprofit organizations that draw on an endowment for the operation of the institution are familiar with this concept. Essentially it is the rate at which the organization is allowed to spend the endowment assets and the investment gains derived from those assets. The best of these groups use a twenty-quarter average of the returns on their assets to set the appropriate spending levels. That span usually encompasses at least one year of negative investment returns. The result for most of these organizations is an annual spending rate of between 4 and 6 percent of the endowment's assets. A higher rate may not be sustainable in each and every year and could therefore force the institution to cut back spending during and after a market decline. Less than 4 percent could mean that during periods of higher-than-normal inflation the institution will suffer a decline in real spending power that might leave some portion of its mission unfulfilled.

These same concepts of fiduciary duty and controlled spending can be applied to personal wealth. For wealthy individuals the equivalent of an endowment is their adjusted net worth. Pay attention, because that word *adjusted* is important. Two adjustments must be made to net worth to derive the proper figure from which to calculate controlled spending. We discussed the first adjustment in chapter 2 which includes not only the cost to fund the rest of your days, but also what you perceive you "owe" to heirs and charities. The second adjustment is the old accounting term *net-net*. The venerable investment text by Graham and Dodd popularized this term as an approach to investing in companies that were priced in the market not only below their net worth, but also without regard to any asset that could not quickly be turned into cash. Few people can count on converting their house or other concrete assets into cash in ninety days or less.

The implication is that if you are rich in land or real estate but cash poor, your spending rate should be based on your liquid assets. This calculation can come as a shock to many, leaving them depressed at the outcome.

"I thought I was rich," you can hear them say. The proper response is "Yes, you are rich, but you are like every other multi-millionaire in that there are some limits on what you can spend over time and still be considered rich."

To oversimplify the spending choices, you can think about whether to be happy you must absolutely have nothing but custom-tailored clothes. Or will off-the-shelf clothing fill some of your needs? Warren Buffett, John Templeton, and Jack Bogle are famous for their parsimonious spending on some items, yet they are truly rich. Getting good value for all that you spend is an important step in controlling your spending rate.

If you are an informal fiduciary or a formal fiduciary for a trust that permits it, you can increase your spending rate by "invading principal," that is, spending at a rate higher than the assets earn and thus eating into the assets themselves. Be forewarned: if you come from a long line of wealth, your long-deceased ancestors will be spinning rapidly in their graves. They amassed that wealth precisely by not invading principal. But a growing number of people of wealth, particularly of sudden wealth, intend to spend every dollar, and if nothing is left for family and heirs, that's fine with them. I have no quarrel with their intention, but I advise such people to set aside a large contingency fund to cover the costs of unexpected developments. A lengthy illness can cost well into six figures.

As an advisor serving wealthy clients, I recognize that my job is to suggest investment patterns that will accomplish most of their objectives most of the time, not all of their objectives all the time. Given a certain tolerance for uncertainty and depending on their spending rate, working together with clients, we can devise an investment program. What their objectives are and how they dispose of their wealth is strictly their decision. Much of this book is about how your goals and your investment psychology will influence the design of your portfolio.

We have talked about greed and fear as motivators and modifiers of investment decisions, but another modifier is seldom noted in the financial-planning community. I pointed out earlier that your network of friends and colleagues is a vital, albeit difficult to value, part of your net worth. Throughout our lives we have been meeting people, many of whom become part of our social network. We often fail to recognize that we share with some of them our financial experiences and hear from them about theirs. We can all learn and gain from these shared experiences, and the more you interact with people or, in some cases, institutions, the more valuable they can become to you. The strength of this network lies in its role as an informal "favor bank." The favors can range from something major, such as helping someone get a job, be nominated to an exclusive club, or get an appointment with a medical or investment professional who is no longer accepting new clients, to the minor, perhaps saving a seat at the local high school baseball game. This favor bank benefits both the depositor and the withdrawer because each interaction brings you closer together. Your network can lead to

interesting investments of both your time and money and has
the salutary effect of enhancing your life while often moderating
your spending. If you do not already have a focus around which
to build your network, think seriously about taking up something
like golf, painting, or a nonprofit endeavor, that will bring you together with like-minded people. The dividends, both psychic
and financial, can be gratifying.

7

THE COST OF LIVING:
Your Personal CPI

0 ne of the most important lessons of investing is to understand the impact of inflation on returns. In times of moderate inflation that impact can be an insidious, almost undetectable decline in the value of one's assets. The total monetary value may rise, but the purchasing power is what matters, and a lengthy span of even modest inflation can do heavy damage to a portfolio's purchasing power if that portfolio isn't properly invested. I needn't go into detail about the impact on values of severe inflation. All this explains the bias toward investing in equity—ownership—as opposed to debt, usually in the form of bonds. One seeks equity ownership in the hope that, on balance, the payoff from those assets will exceed the impact of inflation (as well as, hopefully, taxes). Inflation's impact should be central to your thinking about investing.

What is inflation? One might say that it is the progression of prices either up or down. A decline in prices is called deflation, whereas a decline in the *rate* of inflation is called disinflation. And how is inflation measured? The standard answer is via the measure established by the government. Most people have heard about the Consumer Price Index and use that as their primary measure of inflation without any real understanding of how this measure was created and is calculated. The U.S. Department of Commerce, which collects retail prices and calculates the index, has recognized that its methodology is far from perfect. Analysts and economists understand, for example, that both geography and population density play a role. Prices in some locations move more than prices in other places, and prices in cities tend to be higher than prices in less populous locales. To take those geographical and population effects into account, the department calculates subindexes. One can, for instance, get a calculation of inflation in urban, northeast New Jersey. One of the trickier calculations is the attempt to translate the costs of home ownership into an equivalent rent measure. Few economists and analysts believe that anyone can correctly correlate the costs of home ownership with those of renting each month.

Every few years, in an attempt to keep the CPI current and reasonably parallel to the general experience, the Commerce Department reviews the components—the products and services—that are measured to calculate the CPI. A separate attempt is also made to adjust for the qualitative improvement caused by technology. For many years the Federal Reserve used an additional measure called the deflator, which used other statistical techniques to identify the impact of inflation on our national aggregates.

One of the drivers of prices is the cost of labor. The U.S. Department of Labor collects payroll and survey data on what people are paid. More important in today's globally competitive environment, the Labor Department also calculates a measure of productivity, which roughly estimates the cost of labor per unit of production. Rising labor productivity tends to moderate rises in prices.

But for all its efforts to describe, adjust, and measure the various components that contribute to inflation, the government is still capturing mostly national averages. Think for a moment about going to your doctor for a physical or to have him check for some health problem. How important are the national averages for the population's age, height, and incidence of disease to your doctor's diagnosis of and prescription for your specific problem? Correct, the answer is not at all.

National data on inflation should be of limited importance in driving your investment decisions. A more accurate measure of your personal inflation data will be of much more value to the beneficiaries of your money, including yourself. While the general perception of inflation will drive overall security prices, the value of your portfolio to you is much more dependent upon your own perception of inflation. Thus you need to be aware of your personal CPI.

Despite all the talk we hear about inflation, few people are that conscious of prices. Unless you are the primary food shopper for your household and have a memory for prices of goods and services purchased exactly one year ago, you may not be a good source of inflation data. We all talk generally about the reported real estate prices in our communities, yet we fail to acknowledge that we seldom have any exactly comparable sales from one year ago by which to gauge the changes in home prices. Many of us have become much more conscious of gasoline prices, but most of that attention is focused on regular grade with little thought given to the higher-octane gasoline products used for higher-performance vehicles. For the most part, then, we do not think often or very rationally about inflation's impact on our lives. To become better investors and perhaps better spenders as well, we should become more attuned to the changing prices of goods and especially the services we purchase.

The key to developing your personal CPI is to regularly record prices that are important to you. Since inflation is expressed as a rate or percentage, the best measure is to compare the prices of similar items to their prices one year ago to avoid the impact of seasonal influences. If you wish to get a head start on measuring inflation, particularly "cost push" inflation that occurs as producers incur higher costs to bring you a particular product or service, you might monitor the price of a barrel of West Texas petroleum, or unprocessed coffee. For "demand pull" inflation, that is price increases that result from a rising demand from businesses or consumers for a product or service, you might look at the price of scrap steel as a reasonable indicator on the industrial side of the economy. The cost of labor can be measured by those who are in business by comparing what it costs today to hire a replacement employee to what it cost a year ago for an employee of similar capabilities or with similar credentials.

One of the reasons people seek and enjoy wealth is so that they can hire others to perform tasks for them. That can include food preparation and cleanup, house painting, gardening, etc. We are in effect buying the labor of chefs, maids, gardeners, nannies, and architects. The compensation we pay for these services is set by supply and demand for people's services or alternative uses for their time and talents. For the most part these prices will move coincident with or lag behind general inflationary trends. Hairdresser and barber prices tend to move in at least single-dollar increments. Thus their pattern is much more of a stairstep than a rising curve. The price rises are often late and should be viewed as confirming inflationary trends rather than as leading indicators of inflation. Local competition can influence the timing of the increases (I have never known a barber to cut prices even if his customers come in less frequently).

The things I have just discussed are indicators that you should be watching to get a sense of an overall trend in inflation. To calculate your own CPI the most useful exercise is to compare your spending in the most recent month with that in the same month a year ago after you have excluded any unusual expenses in either month. As with any time series, one data point can be misleading. Three are better, and five fixes a trend. Remember, though, that over a few years it will be common for you to consume more, if not more expensive, services.

No matter how imprecise various measures of inflation may be, whether your own or the government's, you should always be paying attention to inflation. The old saw is that only two things are certain, death and taxes. To that I would add price changes.

While we certainly wish to avoid any encounter with high rates of inflation, we must also realize that prices decline from time to time due to too little demand or an excess of supply. While one might think a period of declining prices would be welcome—the same amount of money buys more!—the periods of multiyear deflation we have endured in the past have been anything but welcome.

8

RESOURCES
AND RESPONSIBILITIES:
Funding Your Liabilities

I n our earlier discussion of your balance sheet we identified both your formal liabilities—mortgages and other
contractual debts—as well as your noncontractual obligations
including retirement; contingent health reserve; children's,
grandchildren's, and possibly great-grandchildren's education;
and charities. You want to be able to match your resources
against the responsibilities you have undertaken.

There are two approaches to matching resources with obligations. The first is to look at the present value of your after-tax
resources (both income taxes and estate taxes). This approach
deals with known facts. A good trust and estate lawyer, and a
tax accountant, become your principal aides in this endeavor.
Converting your assets to cash for spending now and in the defined future can be handled somewhat mechanically without
much in the way of help from your investment advisor(s). Often

multiple advisors and managers can produce better and perhaps safer results.

The second approach begins with several somewhat frightening realizations. First, the future level of your assets is uncertain because of changes in taxes and inflation, which is the same thing as the devaluation of currency. Added to these uncertainties is the virtual certainty that investments won't at all times perform as expected (but you already know this through experience). The second set of realizations comes from our own inability to predict the needs that we wish to fulfill to ourselves, loved ones, and the good works of charities. All of these factors lead us to recognize, first, that our current assets must grow to keep up with the future expected needs of ourselves and others; and second, that like a kid in a candy shop, the totality of our desires exceeds our expected resources. This last realization may cause us to prioritize our desires and eliminate or reduce the financial tasks we can reasonably hope to accomplish. With this second and more realistic approach, one or more investment advisors or managers should play the lead role with strong support from your other two primary advisors.

What financial instruments can you use to fulfill your obligations? I will focus on securities, either individual stocks or bonds, or a collection of securities packaged as funds, which often represent the better choice. Real estate, operating businesses, and other forms of intellectual property as well as some objects of art can and should be substituted for securities with the aid of knowledgeable and trusted advisors. When dealing with assets in which there is no public record of transactions and prices, trust in an "expert" becomes critical. Each of these assets have some bond- and stocklike characteristics and should be slotted in the same asset groupings based on these securities. In most cases the value of these assets should be discounted by some amount because of their illiquid nature and their heavy dependence on specific individual talents. Discounting an illiquid asset as compared to a listed stock that trades a million or more shares a day at prices of $40 would suggest that a private business of similar characteristics should be valued at no more than 65 percent of the public company. If the company is highly dependent upon a single manager or even a small number of talented people, a further discount of 20 percent or thirteen percentage points would reduce the discounted value to approximately 52 percent or some such number. Similar discounting metrics exist for real estate, intellectual property, and works of art. Thus in looking at hard assets of $50 million in freely tradable securities and a similar amount in a private operating business, it would be wise to calculate the total assets not as $100 million that could meet your undertaken obligations but at about $73 million ($50 million + $23 million) pretax and before the cost of disposal. You should not, however, use that same discounting approach when taking into account the income generated from private assets. One might think of that as double discounting. Nevertheless, the predictability of income is an important consideration to be built into your resource analysis.

For most of the wealthy who are no longer involved with full-time (seventy-hours-per-week!) jobs with meaningful compensation, securities are the basic building blocks of their investment portfolios. Unless one is dealing with fraud or gross incompetence, there are no bad securities, just securities with different and better characteristics including current valuations. The securities deemed to be the most creditworthy for U.S. citizens and residents are those issued by the U.S. Treasury. In nominal terms they have never failed to pay interest or to repay principal on time, unlike the debt issued by our government during our revolution. The faith in the creditworthiness of this paper around the world is based on both its history and the taxing power of the government, which is remarkable considering that there has never been an outside audit of the government. Of course, such an audit would not be all that useful since it would not recognize the current value of the government's assets in such things as Western lands and intellectual property or the liabilities of continuing obligations such as open-ended health-related costs. In developing our highest form of certainty we accept only the taxing authority of the U.S. Treasury, not agency paper that is guaranteed by the U.S. government (Congress), which can change its obligations at will. For our financial base we should avoid the temptation to try to improve the income yield by purchasing fixed-income paper from the commercial world or complex securities. Remember that the yield in the marketplace is in proportion to the perceived risk of loss or delay of repayment of interest or capital. The market turmoil of the summer of 2007 reminds us of the absolute need to fully understand the sources of income of what we own. Some investors believed that Collateralized Debt Obligations (CDOs) marketed with AAA ratings were risk-free. They did not understand that these are complex, multilayered collections of different credit levels of debt with at least in some cases the bottom level being made up of some possibly shaky subprime mortgage debt. In funding our liabilities we use U.S. Treasuries to meet principal or contractual obligations. Usually the length of these payments should be short-term. The income from these bills or notes is taxable at the federal level. Further, the principal will lose value to inflation unless you use TIPS, which are largely protected against inflation pretax.

Recognizing that today's dollar will not, in all likelihood, buy the same quantity and probably quality in the future, you need to grow your balance sheet to overcome the effects of inflation, taxes, and other expense payments that stand between you, as grantor, and the beneficiaries of your wealth. The longer the period between the "sip and the lip," the greater the need for capital growth becomes. The greater the need for capital growth, the more uncertain is the result. Historically, in most periods, ownership of equity has produced greater returns than ownership of debt. This need for capital growth has meant most fortunes, defined in your own terms, are invested in ownership. There are some skilled investors in real estate, operating businesses, intellectual property, and artworks. Most of those who are really skilled in investing in these forms do it for their own account and do not expect to find similar talents over generations. By default and practice, the bulk of investments, after the operating-earnings phase of life, are in equity securities.

Investing in securities today has become the province of skilled professionals. Few of these professionals are skilled in managing money in all worthwhile classes of equity. History shows a regular rotation of types of equities that do well and poorly. As the rotation eventually returns to the starting types of equity, not necessarily the same securities, any one form of investing may be as productive as any other, and thus a particular type of manager can succeed. The problem is that no one knows which type of investment and manager will be good for the next period or the one after that. If it is any comfort, a statistical phenomenon known as regression to the mean states that investment classes that are currently outperforming or underperforming their historical average rate of return will eventually return to that average. I should caution you, however, that the dropping in performance rank order from the top has stronger statistical evidence than the rise (from the dead) from the bottom, as some of those securities at or near the bottom will simply disappear.

If your accepted liabilities to yourself, your partner in life, children, grandchildren, great-grandchildren, and others dear to you, plus your intended good works for charity, cover long periods up to and including eternity, you need not only a group of managers who have different investment skills, but also a set of advisors who can properly invest your "aboveground" legacy for people whom you think you know, but may and will in all likelihood change when you are no longer around. Investing for charitable heirs is very different from investing for individuals, but no less challenging. In an ideal world you will have selected a group of managers with great skill in each important type of investment. Perhaps a multibillionaire could have such a stable of experts and coordinators, but the rest of us will have to make compromises with the ideal.

My approach is first to go the fund route, since I recognize that I am not skilled in many or, perhaps on some days, any of the different types of equity needed to accomplish the goals on my balance sheet with high odds of success. These funds can be mutual funds, closed-end funds, hedge funds, and other alternative asset funds. These investment vehicles are managed within certain specified limits in which the manager has full discretion. While most investors first look to determine which assets classes they should invest in, such as large-cap, growth, or emerging-markets funds, I do not. I start looking for skilled managers who have over many time periods demonstrated good relative investment performance in good times and understandable and tolerable performance in bad times. I look for managers who can carefully rotate their portfolio weightings and selections over multiple periods. My bias in most cases is to choose managers with relatively low turnover rates both of securities and, more important, personnel, including those in key noninvestment jobs. Another bias of mine is to go with managers who do enough of their own research to have worthwhile proprietary views on individual securities and sectors. While my primary reliance is on good managers, I do want some diversification of managers to improve the odds that my portfolio will grow most of the time. Markets of all types go from broad participation in which just about every issue rises in price to increasingly narrow markets in which only a few securities are rising in price. I want to participate in most market rises.

Understanding what kinds of environments have been favorable to my stable of good managers, I look for differences among them. While having multiple managers investing in the same type of securities can protect me from the specific risks in the portfolio or, more important, in the manager's organization, too much concentration neglects other portions of the constantly rotating markets. I also look at the type of environment in which different managers tend to do well. For example, so-called value investors have a better opportunity to buy things well in quiet markets with low volatility. They are often buying from investors who need to raise cash to meet some funding requirement. These value investors often find their best environment when other investors give up prematurely on such investment themes as a corporate turnaround, the long-delayed promise of a new product or new management, or an expected change in the investment cycle. These periods do not typically produce good returns for value investors because few investors are willing to buy what the value investor owns. But that period of subpar performance is later more than offset when the scales suddenly drop from the eyes of other investors and they see the value in the company, product, management, or financial season that the value investor foresaw much earlier. These buyers can be market rotators or more likely strategic buyers who want to separate the assets of the company, possibly including talented workers, from their public shareholders. When there are perceived to be a number of strategic buyers, whether true or not, the stocks' assets become competitively priced rather than selling at some discount. These are good performance periods for many of these "value" managers.

In assessing these managers, I look to see how many names in the portfolio change between the buying period and the selling period. There should be some turnover of securities over the years, but not in each and every year. An ideal situation is to see an increase in turnover in exuberant markets mostly driven by sales and some buying at the nadir of markets. If there is not a big change compared to the portfolios of other managers, the resulting portfolio is revealed to be essentially an index fund of what was and may still be cheap stocks. While there may be a place in my stable of managers for such portfolios, they do not deserve a particularly high management fee or total expense ratio. The total expense ratio is the impact of all expenses including management, custodial, transfer-agent, and professional fees. In many separate account relationships only the management fee is obvious; the rest are bundled somewhere else and are not visible. The lack of comparable total expense ratios makes comparisons between funds and separate accounts difficult in the short run.

Other managers have different kinds of good periods, which can be identified by their characteristics: broadening public participation, yield chasing, high innovation excitement, and scarcity of resources and talents, for example. Some of these market environments overlap, which does not help in our diversification efforts, but does give us a clue as to where we are in the petrified-bored-intrigued-excited-exuberant cycle. If too many things are going right, we need to be particularly cautious as there will in time be too many investments going down. Picking managers may be like picking tennis players for a singles tennis team. You want them all to be good, but if you want to win consistently, you will choose players who show particular skills on different surfaces and against certain types of opponents. That is how I suggest that you build your team of good managers.

9

THE FOUR-LETTER WORD:
The Meaning and Causes of *Risk*

Too much has been written and too little understood about one of the most important four-letter words: *risk*. As with many other four-letter words—*love, hate, dear, bond, fast, slow,* take your pick—each of us knows what they mean to us individually, and those meanings vary among us. *Fast* means one thing to someone riding a bike, something else to someone driving a car, and something yet again to someone's behavior. Our personal, intuitive definitions depend on our experience, the context in which the four-letter word is used, and to whom we're speaking. Risk is one of those things we do not consciously think much about in ordinary life. We have learned to live with the risks associated with crossing the street, eating uncooked foods, and even dying before you finish reading this sentence. We deal with these risks unconsciously, without relying on precise numbers or Greek letters. But when we associate risk and money, everything changes. Doubtless you have been exposed to some of the terminology slung around by investment advisors: *risk-free return, beta, value at risk (VAR),* and *volatility index (VIX).* You can blame all that jargon on academics.

The academics had a problem when it came to teaching investing. Plenty of ways existed to measure gains and losses looking backward and using finite numbers that represented past events. Their problem was describing results in the future. The concept of reward in and of itself was not difficult. For centuries people had been getting incentives to invest their wealth or their sweat for gain. But the academics wanted to quantify those future rewards the same way they quantified past rewards. Complicating it all was that the future held not just the possibility of reward, but also the possibility of loss. The academics knew intuitively that losses happened from time to time, but it was difficult to quantify the possibility of loss as a statement of risk. The solution they devised was volatility, the tendency of results to vary from a trend line. Risk, they decided, was represented by the variability of returns. Note that they did not even try to come up with a cause-and-effect relationship, that is, what *caused* the variability. So today we're left with a definition of risk that can be expressed mathematically to many decimal places and used to compare one investment with another. But what we actually have is a confusion of precision with accuracy, where precision is measured to five or more decimal places and accuracy is an insightful understanding of what actually happened.

I believe a much more useful way to think about risk in

making investment decisions is to ask: what is the consequence of being wrong? Under this approach the day-to-day fluctuations in asset values are meaningless. The real risk is being wrong over time to such an extent that the loss of money prevents me from accomplishing one or more of my goals. Under this approach, risk is relative. Take, for example, two investors who own the same relatively stable stock, currently priced at $10, a price that has not changed in three years. One investor has his entire life savings tied up in five thousand shares of the stock. The other investor owns fifty thousand shares, or ten times as much in dollar terms. For the second investor, that represents less than one-half of 1 percent of his total wealth of $100 million. If one day the stock opens not at $10 a share, but at $3 a share, the investor with his life savings tied up in the stock is devastated. The second investor experiences a much larger dollar loss, but in reality it is just a rounding error in his overall wealth. As a result of this shift in the value of a share of stock, the first investor has suddenly lost many opportunities—the ability to buy a car, send his daughter to college, or pay off his mortgage. He probably will sell in a panic, thus locking in his loss, and he may never buy another share of any stock as long as he lives, thereby missing out on a huge opportunity for amassing wealth. Thus we see that the risk of loss is attached not to the security itself, but to the investor.

Having been around investors for most of my life, I have observed four root causes that lead people to take risks large enough to be life-altering: overconfidence, personality change, leverage, and unanticipated events. Let us take a closer look at each of these.

OVERCONFIDENCE

People with wealth are particularly susceptible to this root cause of risk. They believe they have so much money that a loss here or there—much like that of our second investor above—will have little or no impact on their lives. I think of it as the "Maginot Line syndrome." In the early stages of World War II the French were confident that their interlinked line of robust forts and powerful guns would prevent the Germans from conquering France. The Germans merely did an end run and seized France by coming in through Belgium, demonstrating a remarkable case of French overconfidence.

Closer to home, we may be witnessing another case of over-confidence if we look at the New York Yankees and their fans' assumption at the beginning of each season that the Yanks will win that year's World Series. That confidence is even reflected in monetary terms if we look at the bonds issued by the Yankees and their crosstown rival the Mets to build new stadiums, both scheduled to open in 2009. The older and better-known Yankees got a more favorable rate and raised more money than did the Mets. The logical assumption one might make is that the Yankees simply have the upper hand financially and can afford better talent with a better chance of winning the Series. Maybe, maybe not. Only time will tell whether that confidence is really over-confidence.

Many wealthy investors tend to behave much like the French generals and the Yankee fans. They feel secure behind their fortress of money and find it difficult to accept that they may be

wrong. Perhaps dreadfully wrong. If pushed, they might acknowledge the possibility that either they or their advisors could be
wrong at some point, but they seldom build a mechanism to
handle the occurrence of a mistake, learn from the mistake, recover from it, and even profit from it. In contrast, the only thing
I promise the investors in our accounts is that I will be wrong
from time to time and hope to learn from the mistake, and that
I manage in a way that can ultimately benefit them.

PERSONALITY CHANGE

We are all too human, which means we change over time. Those
changes result in the second major source of risk to our wealth:
personality change. *Personality* is a catchall word that can include
any number of traits and a huge variety of emotional and rational
states of mind. Some common traits that define a personality include "friendly," "optimistic," and "energetic." Some emotional
states of mind are "angry" and "frightened" and "happy." Rational
states of mind are described as "logical," "meticulous." The various combinations of traits and states of mind make us who we
are at any given time. But because those combinations can change
in myriad ways and for unforeseen reasons, we may be someone
very different a few years from now than we are today. And the
same changes can take place in the people who surround us, including our loved ones, our friends, our advisors, and the man-
agements of the entities in which we invest. The changes, both in
us and in those around us, have important implications for our financial futures.

Most of the change that takes place in our personalities over time stems from our changing physical, emotional, and mental health, all conditions over which we have limited control. But our personalities are also influenced, perhaps move heavily than we realize, by significant changes in our financial condition, either for better or for worse. Consider how different individuals might react to essentially flat returns in their investment portfolios over a sustained time. One person might be relieved not to have suffered any losses, while another is upset at not keeping pace with inflation, while a third is deeply envious of friends whose portfolio values have substantially risen over the same period. The resulting emotions can prompt us to question the strength of our convictions and, worse, to take actions such as spending less or restructuring our investments. Why worse? Because it is a reaction to the past, not a view to the future.

Similar changes in those around us can prompt the same kinds of changes. Is our son-in-law frustrated in his high-paying, high-stress job and thinking of changing careers? What he does may cause you to become more nervous about your daughter's financial future. Is your chief financial advisor becoming more conservative as she grows older? Is she less interested in the day-to-day drudgery of managing her clients' portfolios and more interested in being her firm's "rainmaker"? Changes like that take place over time and can be hard to detect until some event brings home to you that your financial advisor is not being as attentive to your financial needs as you think she should be. Is your favorite charity shifting the focus of its resources in ways that you do not feel appropriate? Your attitude toward the charity will likely change long before your giving practices do.

If you are like most people, your needs will change over time along with your personality. Typically, people want to increase their own standard of living, they want to do more to help their loved ones, whether aging parents or children and grandchildren, and they often want to do more charitable giving. Unless you are committed to a strict budget, most of those changes mean spending more, which can be accomplished in different ways. Perhaps you have the discipline to reduce spending on yourself and reallocate that money to your other needs. Some may seek to generate more money by shifting assets to generate higher expected returns. But those higher returns come at a price: risk. And with increased risk comes reduced comfort as the margin of safety over your spending needs shrinks. Noble purposes often drive investors to take more risk than they would find comfortable if they were selfishly thinking only of their own needs. The key question then becomes, can your personality accept the higher risks and the possible long-term consequences?

The best way to deal with the pressures of trying to meet your perceived obligations to others is to ensure that their expectations are realistic and based on the way you are thinking about your obligations to them. Too few people have those kinds of discussions, fearful that changing circumstances and financial conditions will alter their ability to later meet commitments that they make now. You can overcome those fears by avoiding making specific dollar-amount commitments. Instead, be sure everyone understands that you will allocate your resources to them based on a program of percentages, which may include tiers and even sunset provisions. By stating that any one person or organization will receive a certain percentage of your estate rather than a stipulated dollar amount, you reduce your burden to fulfill what you may perceive as a contract that does not allow you to change your mind. Another approach is to annually reallocate both your resources and your planned dispositions. In either case, particularly during periods of inflation, keep the maximum amount of your assets in equities of various types.

In the end we are all at risk both to ourselves and to others. Being aware of those risks and how they change over time allows us to make the kinds of judicious decisions that minimize the impact of those risks.

LEVERAGE

The third root cause of dangerous levels of risk is leverage. There are many forms of leverage, but let's begin by thinking about the nature of leverage in terms of elementary physics. Remember the teeter-totter we discussed earlier? Whether in your backyard or in the local park, the fun of the teeter-totter lay in a close balance between you and the kid on the other end. You push off from the ground and your partner at the other end plunges downward, only to absorb the fall and push off to send you plunging. But what happens if you suddenly roll backward off your seat when you are at the bottom? Your friend plunges without any counterbalancing weight and may wind up hurt. That scenario illustrates leverage: using leverage can help you rise on the weight and efforts of others, but it can also result in a painful drop if the other side defaults.

In the financial world, two forms of leverage concern us. The first is *operating leverage,* undertaken by the companies or governments in which we invest. The second is *financial leverage,* which we engage in to boost our investment returns. Operating leverage is a simple concept that has led to the creation of many fortunes. When a company, whether engaged in services or manufacturing, collects enough revenue to cover its fixed expenses, the remaining revenue falls to the bottom line as profit after paying for the variable expenses. A company that can increase revenue while holding the line on costs enjoys tremendous benefits from operating leverage. As investors or entrepreneurs we love to find opportunities to benefit from operating leverage. Our preference for these kinds of businesses tends to make them expensively priced on the market. The problem is that a decline in sales to a level below expenses, especially rising expenses, can cause a precipitous plunge in profits and result in an even more precipitous share-price decline for investors in the company. If we invest only in companies that enjoy operating leverage or, to put it another way, expanding profit margins, we are exposing ourselves to a dangerous degree to an overall slowing of economic growth. Prudent portfolios balance such exposure with investments that are not exclusively dependent on overall economic growth.

Much more dangerous to many investors and entrepreneurs is financial leverage, which, in its simplest form, is the use of someone else's assets to grow your own, usually through borrowing. The most common example is a mortgage loan, which allows us to make a minimum investment of our own money to control an asset—a house—by borrowing a large amount to finance the purchase. While banks are the most common source of financial leverage, more sophisticated sources are available, including the issuance of notes or bonds. The danger in financial leverage is that the entity from which you borrow money can, under certain circumstances, demand rapid repayment on terms and at a time that is most inconvenient. The demand for repayment may force the borrower to dispose of other assets quickly and under unfavorable terms. A margin call from a stockbroker, for example, can force an investor to liquidate other assets within hours to meet the call. In a time of economic uncertainty or decline, the forced sale of desirable investments in a time of rapidly declining asset prices can be extremely painful.

Put in more personal terms, if a person or company owes you something and suddenly and unexpectedly cannot deliver, you become at risk to meet your own scheduled payments. On a large scale, economists call this systemic risk. This exposure can be created by misjudgment, rumor, fraud, or all three together. If all three elements occur simultaneously, the result can be a devastating panic that sweeps through financial markets, such as the 20 percent collapse in stock prices in one day in 1987.

While there is no absolute protection against the ravages of a financial panic, some techniques can mitigate the effects. First is to diversify into assets that are not correlated, that is, assets that do not move in the same direction at the same time, which means that the other owners are not likely to own any of the plunging securities. That is simple to say, much more difficult to achieve. When Russia defaulted on its treasury bills, stocks in Latin America and elsewhere plunged, a correlation that surprised many professional investors and traders. What was the connection? When trading desks and other proprietary traders who were using borrowed money realized that part of their portfolio was suddenly virtually worthless, they needed to raise money to meet their margin calls. The smart ones had learned from previous crises that they could raise that money fastest by selling their best assets. The resulting decline in prices of assets around the globe came to be called emerging-market contagion. The history of finance is one of defending against known risks, only to be blindsided by unanticipated or unforeseeable events.

You can protect yourself against a collapse from financial leverage by diversifying the array of financial advisors you choose. There doubtless is a place within your portfolio of advisors and agents for an aggressive manager, and an equally important place for a more conservative manager. Having a manager with a non-U.S. portfolio can help offset a manager who focuses strictly on U.S. investments. For those with sufficient wealth, the best way to protect against the risk of systemic problems is to employ, either directly or through a financial advisor, a group of experienced credit researchers. While I have a great deal of respect for the well-known credit-rating agencies, their strength lies in conventional analysis of the ability of issuers to make timely repayment of principal and interest, not in the ability to predict bond prices or, more importantly, derivative prices. As we have seen, the problems that lead to systemic risk often arise from unconventional, unanticipated, and even bizarre events.

The real problem with any form of leverage is that its successful use becomes habit-forming and its dangers tend to fade from sight. The smartest business and investment operators that I know periodically review their portfolios with an eye toward deleveraging. In essence, they are renewing their knowledge that leverage can be dangerous. Additionally, they rarely come close to maximizing their leverage, choosing instead to create a margin of safety against the possibility of a rapidly deteriorating market. While we all are leveraged to some degree, the key to avoiding big risks is to identify our risks and use periods of exuberance when rising asset prices dominate the cocktail-party chatter to cut back on our exposure. The key to fulfilling our long-term goals and obligations lies as much in surviving problems as enjoying profits.

UNANTICIPATED EVENTS

The fourth major source of investment risk is unanticipated events. Of the four major sources of investment risk in this discussion, we have a measure of control over three: overconfidence, personality change, and leverage. But in the face of unanticipated events, we are virtually helpless. By definition, an unanticipated event was not only not planned for, but was not even contemplated. When we buy life insurance or home insurance we do so because we think the insurance industry, with its voluminous actuarial tables and immense database of previous occurrences, knows precisely what risks we face and has priced its products to be certain that should an isolated "unanticipated event" strike one of its clients, the funds provided by all the others through premium payments will be adequate to pay for the resulting loss. Certainly the insurance industry sings that song, both to us as buyers of insurance and to investors who buy the insurance companies' shares. They may even believe it themselves because of the favorable past experiences they and their competitors have had in accepting the specific risks on our homes and lives. Yet I cannot tell you how many times as a securities analyst I have seen insurance companies that have suffered underwriting losses due to an unanticipated increase in morbidity (deaths) or the occurrence of a "hundred-year storm." One tragic example is the life underwriters who wrote policies on young people in the 1980s just as the AIDS epidemic was about to burst on the scene.

What has happened is that we as individual insurance buyers have transferred our specific risks to a "pool" operator who admittedly has better odds working for him. But neither we as a collection of individuals nor the pool operator have eliminated risk. Instead, we have simply transformed it by breaking it into small parts of a large pool. No amount of actuarial studies or statistical manipulations can eliminate risk. If professional insurance underwriters can fall victim—admittedly, again, only occasionally—to unanticipated events, we as investors in much less certain securities can certainly expect to fall victim to unanticipated events. That risk should be acknowledged in our investment philosophy and personality. To paraphrase a common quip, "We know what we do not know and we don't know what we do not know."

To handle this risk of unanticipated events, Ben Graham and David Dodd, the latter a professor of mine at Columbia, developed in their seminal work *Security Analysis* the concept of "margin of safety." They looked for securities that were selling substantially below their current value. The difference between the purchase price of the security and its higher intrinsic value became, in effect, a reserve against the risk that an unanticipated event would lower the price that a knowledgeable buyer would pay for more seriously damaged merchandise. We should follow a similar practice. The trick lies in determining how large the margin of safety needs to be to cover potential losses that would result from an unanticipated event. But unanticipated events do not necessarily result in losses. They can just as easily result in gains. Determining the size of the valuation reserve for an unanticipated event forces us not only to recognize the near certainty of the existence of unknowns, but also to judge what we can afford to lose when the event occurs. In other words, how wrong can we be and how much will it cost us and how much do we care? Consider the different reactions of the two shareholders we discussed earlier who in one day experienced a 70 percent decline in the value of one stock.

Many investors tend to overestimate the negative impact of an unanticipated event. I will use elections as an example. Every time a national election occurs, the media has the requisite story about what investors expect and how the stock or bond market will react. Those stories are almost always overly hyped and often just plain wrong. In November 2004, I did not anticipate that two years later the Republicans would lose not only control of both houses of the U.S. Congress, but also the majority of state governor posts. I daresay most other investors also expected a continuation of Republican control for some time. I was wrong. So was the conventional wisdom that a Democratic sweep of Congress would result in a sharp decline in stock prices. Indeed, in the immediate aftermath of the elections the stock market rose. This illustrates that the thing to keep foremost in our minds is not the nature of the unanticipated event itself, but its financial impact. As we try to come to grips with the risks to our investment portfolio from unanticipated events, we should think not about some precise numbers, but instead about our own comfort level.

My own rough rule of thumb calls for a 25 percent decline in the U.S. stock market in some twelve-month period during every ten calendar years, and a 50 percent decline once in each generation, or roughly twenty-five years. My rule of thumb applies only to the stocks of large, well-capitalized companies and not to thinly traded over-the-counter securities or to stocks that are primarily traded overseas. In both those latter cases, the declines—and gains—can and probably will be larger. The distinction that I am making is that as long as the major U.S. markets maintain floor specialists and a significant number of well-capitalized market makers, there will be sufficient liquidity for most investors to cushion the declines. When there are few or, in the worst case, no well-capitalized buyers, stock prices will fall to depressed levels much lower than those contemplated in my rule of thumb. Unfortunately, the reduction of share trading by specialist firms on the floor of the NYSE that has resulted from the emergence of various hybrid electronic trading systems is likely to result in increased volatility on "crisis" days. At the same time, the growth of these "upstairs traders," who are not obligated to trade as are the floor specialists, may result in increased intraday volatility on normal days. The severe cutback in the number of specialists and other brokers on the floor is likely to affect the quality of executions, particularly on crisis days. These changes in trading systems may, in the long term, affect my rule of thumb.

10

BAD THINGS HAPPEN:
Taming and Managing Risk

Now that we know some of the root causes of risk to our wealth, the next logical question is how to avoid those risks. The simple answer is that we cannot avoid them completely all the time. A lot of people talk about "risk avoidance," but the more realistic approach is to talk about "risk assumption." In other words, just assume that there is risk and do what you can to reduce the effects should something go wrong. Perhaps that is easier said than done because we're all creatures of habit and tend, over time, to quit thinking excessively about risk. Over the years we learn that some actions we take produce positive results, while other actions produce negative results. We assume that the next time we take a similar action we will get a similar result. While that usually happens, the result is seldom guaranteed and could be exactly opposite of what we expect.

The opportunity for loss—risk, in short—is pervasive, but we tend to ignore it as much as possible.

Risk assumption requires you to come to grips with the indisputable fact that bad things happen. Our best general defense against these bad things lies in understanding the odds that something bad will happen and then taking whatever steps we can to improve our odds. Fortunately, it is easier to calculate the odds and improve them in finance than in almost any other human undertaking. First, we have a massive amount of data in the form of price movements over a long periods for a large number of securities prices. Second, we tend to measure outcomes in a single dimension, that is either up or down from some preexisting point. That is unlike other important aspects of our lives, such as the impact of health on our quality of life or success in our occupations, which provides psychic gratification.

The best defense against overconfidence, one of the biggest risks to our wealth, is simple. Seek the counsel of people who have a history of contrary opinion that has, more often than not, turned out to be right. In other words, find smart people who disagree with you and pay attention to what they're saying and why. Let them challenge your opinions and assumptions. I do not mean you have to go out and find a money manager who constantly knocks down your ideas and argues with you. Rather, find a wide array of opinion by reading about wealth management in such places as *The Wall Street Journal,* the *Financial Times,* or *Barron's.* As a backup you should also seek out well-meaning people who, whether they realize it or not, are wrong most of the time. You're basically looking for a negative indicator. Such negative indicators are not easily found among professional advisors since many of them do not stay in business for long or at least have a hard time attracting media attention, but family members and friends can sometimes be a good source. A good negative indicator, while rare, should be cherished.

The second approach against overconfidence is to lay out a significant number of milestones that your portfolio should achieve. Basically, you are making predictions and setting goals that, if reached, precipitate at least some thought about making changes. If the predictions do not come true or the goals are not met in a defined period, you should become less confident of the position. Not all of the milestones have to be quantitative. Some of the most telling are qualitative in nature, such as a change in the CEO of a company, an important product announcement, a change in a company's reputation for better or worse, or a development involving regulators or competitors that shines a new light on an investment. Falling short of one milestone does not send an automatic "sell" order. But the failure to hit a series of milestones suggests that you may be wise to abandon or meaningfully reduce the size of your emotional and financial commitment.

I realize how difficult it can be to counter overconfidence. Because U.S. stocks have outperformed U.S. bonds during most periods, I'm tempted to recommend to clients that they own a portfolio heavily loaded with equities as I do. However, I'm also aware of at least one calendar year and probably more rolling twelve-month periods in which fixed-income securities did better than stocks. So while the odds favor stocks, I tend to have and to recommend only that the majority—admittedly the vast majority in some cases—of investments in a portfolio be stocks with a small portion in bonds, preferably U.S. Treasury bonds, and in high-quality institutional money-market funds. Even though I have an abiding faith in the future performance of stocks, I do hedge against what may be overconfidence.

A second major cause of risk is unanticipated events. I'm sure you are wondering how you are supposed to anticipate unanticipated events. Anticipating the unanticipated seems logically impossible. But I disagree. While we cannot anticipate any specific unanticipated event, we can be mindful of the lessons of history. Unanticipated events tend to occur in clusters, and there may be some unusual causal connection between them. Thus anytime an unusual physical or financial event occurs, it should trigger an alarm that prompts you to begin scanning the horizon for other signs of danger. The event could be a so-called hundred-year storm, a sudden epidemic, or a string of bankruptcies among companies most people thought were sound. We've already discussed the global shock wave that followed Russia's default on its government debt, and anyone building a house six months after Hurricane Katrina devastated the Gulf Coast knows what happened to the price of construction materials. Just because there have not been any sizable unanticipated events does not mean you can relax. Since they tend to come in clusters, there can be long spans in which nothing happens. The very absence of significant unanticipated events should prompt you to be on guard. If it had been ninety-nine years since the last Category 5 hurricane, I would certainly be alert to the possibility of one soon, particularly if I lived on the Florida coast. What we can be reasonably certain of is that the serious unanticipated event will occur at the most inopportune time for us.

While most people do not think much about fraud and its impact on their wealth, it, too, is an unanticipated event that can wreak havoc. Human nature seems to drive some otherwise upstanding people to surreptitiously "borrow" other people's assets. While in some cases the purloined assets are used for riotous living, most of the time among "professionals" the purpose behind the theft is to cover losses before they are discovered. If the perpetrators are successful, the "theft" will seldom be noticed. But more professionals than you would like to know are tripped up by some unanticipated event that undoes their plot. Fraud is most likely to occur during periods of high volatility and heavy leverage. Seldom are there multiple conspirators. The perpetrator is usually a single actor who, because he or she has come to be regarded as a "trusted" player, is not closely supervised. You have only two somewhat successful defenses against the serious impact on fraud in your own account. The first is the equivalent of a surprise audit. Just show up and try to follow all the way through how your transactions and accounts are handled. Where are the checks and balances? The second approach is to divide your assets among a number of advisors and custodians.

While those moves afford protection for a large portion of your wealth, it still does not guard against what the regulators call a fraud against the market. Because each security in the market is, at least in theory, competing for your dollars, a security that is significantly and fraudulently overpriced will affect many other securities. A stock that achieves high performance through fraud creates the impression that other stocks are "cheap" in comparison. Using the arbitrage theory of pricing, investors purchase these "cheap" stocks when they are, in fact, overpriced.

They only look cheap. And it is not only investors who are defrauded. The managers of the companies with "cheap" stocks may take actions to try to elevate their stock prices based on the false perception created by the fraudulent stock. The steps to elevate their stock prices may be bad long-term decisions for their companies.

An obvious case of fraudulent behavior affecting other companies and investors was WorldCom. Not only did WorldCom devastate its shareholders and seriously hurt its bondholders, it dragged other telecom stocks higher in the telecom bubble. Perhaps the biggest victim was AT&T and its shareholders. The executives of the older and larger company could not believe WorldCom's fabulous results, but felt that they had to follow suit in their sales and service strategies. AT&T relied on the veracity of WorldCom's audited numbers, which were fraudulent. When WorldCom's stock went down, AT&T and other telecom stock prices declined simultaneously. The fraud was not anticipated by either the overall market or WorldCom's competitors. About the only way to have headed off the problem was to pay attention to the adage, if it seems too good to be true, it probably is!

In today's world of interconnectivity and split-second communications, the mere rumor of an unanticipated event can dramatically move markets. Even if a harmful rumor proves to be false, security prices seldom fully recover immediately from the resulting losses. The mere fact that people believed the rumor, albeit for a limited time, suggests in the minds of some that such a calamity could happen and that the chance of such a decline should therefore be incorporated into the price.

A third source of major risk is personality change, whether in ourselves or in others. While a change is not necessarily good or bad, change is an invitation to probe deeper. If your banker, broker, law firm, or accountant switches your account person from John to Jane, the change in personnel is clear, although it does raise some questions. Why was the change made? Could it be that John got promoted and Jane is a rising star? But could it be that John was having performance problems and needed to be replaced? Or the change could be the result of the firm's winning a big new client that required John's expertise, thus signaling a change in your relative importance to the advisor. In any event, unless you already know the new person well, do not give him or her the same trust and latitude for decisions that you gave the predecessor, at first.

Much more difficult to assess is a change in the personality of a person. Your contact is still John, but maybe you notice that "John does not seem himself." We all go through phases in our lives, probably more than we realize. If you spot some changes, you would be wise to treat the new personality as a new person and requalify the person for the job.

Perhaps the most difficult personality change to spot and deal with is our own. Many of us will be unaware of a change until the impact becomes clear. How do you spot these changes? First, your friends and family start to treat you differently. Although they may not say anything to you, they have noticed a change. A doctor may notice something different. Perhaps the best tip-off is if your appearance changes in subtle or substantial ways. These changes may be superficial or an indication of basic changes of thinking or new important influences. A clue to important changes is when your investment priorities change. Anything that causes a 10 percent or more shift in assets suggests a fundamental change. At that point your entire plan, including your will and any trusts, should diligently be reviewed. One reason people use irrevocable trusts is to prevent some of these personality changes from affecting the assets under trust. An irrevocable trust, which has estate-tax advantages, prohibits the grantor from making any changes once the document is signed, offering beneficiaries the advantage of a degree of certainty. But that certainty may become a disadvantage to the grantor if financial conditions change.

The bottom line for most of us is that people—family, friends, or advisors—and our own mental and physical health are more important influences on how we view our financial situation than numbers by themselves.

The final major cause of risk generation is leverage, both your own and that of the parties with which you deal. You can do little about leverage taken on by your institutional or individual counterparties beyond diversifying your portfolios among different managers. But you can monitor your own leverage and credit exposure. As with many investment quantities, it is not the absolute size of the pile of dollars that is exposed, but their proportional representation and importance in your portfolio, particularly your assets that can be converted into cash in three days or less. A million-dollar margin loan is of some interest, but not significance, compared to a well-diversified stock portfolio of $100 million. The importance of the loans becomes paramount when the equity in the account is $800,000 and is invested in three speculative, thinly traded stocks. The critical factor to remember when assessing the risk of leverage is that timing is not often of your own choosing. The margin loan is called, the size of the float drops, or the derivative contract expires, and you face a forced closing of your leveraged position. To keep the risk of leverage contained, I recommend that margin loans be restricted to no more than 25 percent of the diversified portfolio and that only 90 percent of a managed client float be utilized. I know that sounds complicated and it is. If you do not understand these concepts, you should only invest in a cash account for your securities purchases.

Often investors become addicted to the use of leverage and use it constantly, in ever more allegedly "sophisticated" fashions and with more money. The odds are that such an addiction will eventually lead to large losses. Just as with home mortgages, most investors should amortize their borrowings over time and eventually be out of debt, even if it is only temporarily. He who has substantial reserves and borrowing power in times of tumult becomes king of the jungle. Crises will occur from time to time, and for the well prepared, those crises can be the basis for a first, second, or third fortune.

11

EXPECTATIONS:
Coming Face-to-Face with Reality

A discussion of risk and risk management is a good foundation for sharing my thoughts about expectations, or what I prefer to call expectation systems. To review briefly, risk is the penalty for being wrong to the extent that large losses change dramatically the chances of missing one or more important goals. Further, I have already identified the four principal causes of large-scale losses: overconfidence, unanticipated events, personality change, and leverage.

Investment consultants often describe a manager or a firm of managers as either top-down or bottom-up. Those are short-hand terms to contrast whether investment selection starts with a broad view of the universe of available investments or starts with intensely detailed analysis of critical minutiae of a company's business. Few successful long-term investors that I know use one approach to the extreme of totally ignoring the other.

In today's world of hyperventilated marketing, how things "look" is often more important than how things work. The merchandising of soap and cars are cases in point. I think of this as the "optics" approach to marketing. Applying the optics approach to expectations is a useful exercise in thinking about the determination of the future. To put it in simpler terms, one's view will be colored by which optical instrument one is using, a telescope or a microscope. A wise investor uses both along with an understanding of risk of large loss to build a series of simple expectations into more complex expectation systems. In using one of the astronomical telescopes that Caltech uses to scan the skies, a small error in positioning the observer can mean an inaccurate measurement of billions of miles. The degree of error in looking through a microscope may cause a miscalculation on the order of the breadth of a single strand of human hair. The instruments one uses influence both the error rate in results and the initial expectations. The salespeople among us will tend to favor the broad picture that can quickly be communicated by using the telescope for a top-down presentation. The analysts who revel in details will search for clues to the future by ceaselessly sifting information in search of the single gold nugget that leads to the seam of gold that justifies a full-scale mining operation. Most of my fellow analysts subscribe to the bottom-up approach, i.e., the microscope, and therefore in many cases miss the big picture. They are well-trained deductive thinkers, while the salespeople are often inductive thinkers jumping from one generalized point to another, always conscious that the need to communicate effectively usually means to communicate quickly. Both skill sets are useful for successful long-term investors.

Expectations are views about the future. The problem for us is that we have to deal with many futures—tomorrow, the next day, next year, five years, the next election cycle, the period between now and when funds are needed, our own lifetime and the lifetimes of our heirs and their heirs. The future is measured in time periods, some flexible, some fixed. Most of these periods are not related except that they usually start with the present. Therefore, expectations do not have to be related, and it might be foolish to attempt to make them so. For example, in early December of a given year an investor would be wise to believe that the remainder of the year will follow the current trend. Even though there may be a reversal in some relatively minor direction, the odds do not favor a complete investment cycle of a significant decline and substantial recovery before New Year's Eve.

While investment trends may last for years, or even decades, they do not last forever. Hence the oft-quoted cautionary axiom on Wall Street that "trees do not grow to the sky." A major reversal will, in time, end with yet another major change in direction. If the current period is exuberant, individual stock or sector returns could be 20 to 100 percent in a year or less. But if the forecast period is long enough, the odds on price declines will be strong, with perhaps brutal sell-offs that drive some shares down 25, 50, 95, or even 100 percent. (Analytically, I search for multiple periods of declines, actual or relative. Once these periods are found, the size of future declines, absolute or relative, can be forecaste with some caution. The strength of the forecast will be aided if the causes of the decline can be identified and perhaps tracked.)

Combining the up periods with the down periods shows an average volatility-of-return range of up or down about 10 percent annually. U.S. diversified equity mutual funds have produced low-double-digit annual returns for periods as long as thirty-five years. Anyone who follows the market daily probably knows that most stocks do not move more than 1 percent per day, although some do. Those gains or losses are then often largely reversed within five trading days. The result is that the average daily price change cannot be multiplied by five to get the average weekly move, or by two hundred to get a good fix on the annual movement of prices. The message in all of this is that reversals are normal and should be expected the longer a period lasts. Further, some reversals will be partial, and others will be complete, that is, larger than the original up leg.

Many different time periods are important to our expectation setting. They range from very short—today's closing prices—to very long, such as the lifetimes of heirs and their heirs. Not only is expectation setting a function of the impact of achieved or failed expectations, but also of the tools used to generate the expectations. There is a significant difference between a forecast and an expectation. Most forecasts are replayed selections from history for which there is a strong, but not perfect, statistical record. These records can be massaged to produce a precise number with many digits to the right of the decimal point (3.1416 percent). But such a precise forecast confuses precision with accuracy. One can accurately say only that the U.S. stock market rises more years than not. Any statement more precise can be disregarded as unstable.

We set expectations for time periods that will probably

require us to take actions. We may have the rest of today's trading session to complete a desired purchase or sale of a block of stock. Any expectation we set for the completion of that transaction involves looking at the range of prices and volumes today and over the last few days. If our transaction involves a large amount of stock, we might also consider the relative volume of trading of big blocks of stock over the last few days or, in some cases, months and so far today. This approach can be used in large and liquid stocks as well as some of our better investments, which "trade by appointment." That phrase indicates that the stock in question typically has low trading volume, ranging from a few trades per day to some with only a few trades per week. Some of our best investments trade less than a thousand shares a day, e.g., Berkshire Hathaway or a small financial services stock in a small foreign country. Note, however, that these expectations are reached in the course of a "normal" trading day. If breaking news causes a significant price and volume disruption, the study of recent price and volume ranges will no longer be useful.

Another short-term period that can be important to our expectations might be the end of the tax year, to recognize unrealized losses or gains. Expectation setting here is similar to the setting for the end of the trading day in that there is a hard close at a known time and date. (As we move increasingly toward a twenty-four-hour trading day, the end price will most likely be determined not through a "hard" close, but through the use of some accounting conventions.) But expectations are harder to set for end-of-the-year trading because other investors are doing the same thing, thus crowding the market in search of good execution. In short, trading on December 31 will not be "normal," and thus it is less useful to look at the trading trend of the day. That is why, for practical purposes, the end of the taxable year for mutual funds is the end of October. For many "trust banks" and other institutional managers who want to avoid any last-minute administrative tie-up, their last trading day of the year is before Christmas and can be as early as the middle of the month. This is particularly true for the transfer of appreciated securities to a charity, most of which convert these gifts to cash immediately upon receipt.

For most of us long-term expectations are more important than short-term expectations. Some of these periods have reasonably certain termination dates, such as the need to pay educational expenses, a mythical retirement date, or the funding of various charitable needs. Others are more indefinite, such as the number of years to complete college, date of death, or the final settlement of an estate. Since the precise termination date is not known, expectations have to be of a more general nature similar to finding that "normal" trading day.

Still other expectation setting may involve such elements as the impact of politics. Often when investors invest outside their own country, they believe the economic and financial results experienced will largely be a function of government policies. Thus a change of political leadership becomes a critical element to determine investment policy. In the United States many believe that the up and down trends of the markets are linked to the presidential cycle. Investors should take into account a possible change of leadership when setting expectations out more than four years or longer than the remaining term of office for the incumbent president.

We cannot end our discussion of expectations without discussing the unexpected. Briefly put, one must expect that the unexpected will occur. When the unexpected will occur is obviously anyone's guess. The totally unexpected could occur at the personal level, perhaps with the dissolution of your marriage or the sudden death of your spouse, or more painfully a child. Or it could happen at the macroeconomic level in the form of a massive market collapse or as steadily escalating inflation over years that slowly destroys the purchasing power of the investment portfolio. Little can be done to prepare for a specific unexpected event (a prenuptial agreement, buy-sell agreements among partners or firms, and up-to-date wills might be useful in mitigating the impact of some unexpected events), but a lot can be done to prepare for the inevitable surprise that will come from the occurrence of an unexpected event.

Begin by questioning the certitude of your beliefs. If something is believed to be inevitable—stock prices will climb 10 percent per year on average for the rest of an expected lifetime—you are probably being set up for potential shock. Probable, yes, but inevitable? Absolutely not. Second, be sure that your plans have flexibility, the more the better. Diversity is a highly useful form of flexibility in investing, but to provide a degree of protection against whatever unexpected event occurs, that diversity needs to be extensive, going beyond a range of stocks and bonds to include foreign securities and a wide range of alternative investments. Finally, live in a manner so as not to overcommit to fixed expenses that cannot easily be shed. If income from whatever sources comfortably exceeds outflow, you have an established cushion to protect against years of financial pain in the event of a cataclysmic shock to the financial system.

To get a far more complete view of the role of the unexpected, obtain a copy of *The Black Swan* by Nassim Nicholas Taleb, who appropriately holds the title of Dean's Professor in the Sciences of Uncertainty at the University of Massachusetts at Amherst. The title reflects that for centuries in the Old World, people were convinced that all swans were white. After all, no one had ever seen one of another color, a classic case of conventional wisdom. This delusion lasted among Europeans until Australia was discovered and for the first time Europeans cast their eyes on black swans. As Taleb points out, "One single observation can invalidate a general statement derived from millennia of confirmatory sightings of millions of white swans." A black swan in Taleb's construct is a highly improbable event that is unpredictable, has a massive impact, and, in the aftermath, seems less random and more predictable than it was.

Without intending to, in this discussion, we have confused forecasting and expectations. Forecasting is an intellectual manipulation of factors to come to a prediction. In the corporate world, alternative forecasts are created by the changing of the weights of the elements that go into them. Expectations are what we really believe about the future, and they often influence or even control our emotions. Forecasts, to be useful to us, should be seen through the same filters that govern our approach to risk management, that is, guarding against overconfidence, unanticipated events, personality change, and leverage, all of which are intellectual inputs. But an important emotional input exists that

I call the foxhole factor. Soldiers huddling in their foxholes as artillery shells rain down around them often believe that while others around them may be hit, they won't be. This emotional shield prevents them from panicking at the thought of near-certain death. While our investment expectations are not nearly so dramatic, the lesson we learn from the foxhole factor is that after we apply all of our logical inputs to a forecast, it is how we feel about it that colors our expectations.

12

BOUNCING BACK:

The Art of Recovering from Mistakes

T he logic is inexorable: I am human. Humans make mistakes. Therefore I will continue to make mistakes.

Few areas of life are as susceptible to mistakes as finance and investing. Partly that is the result of their immense complexity. Even the most sophisticated practitioners, including Nobel laureates, can make huge and costly mistakes as was painfully evident in the collapse in 1998 of Long-Term Capital Management and more recently in the debacle triggered by the widespread use of subprime mortgages to chase high returns. But mistakes also arise out of the usual human frailties: inattention, hubris, the desire to be liked, and the desire to avoid pain, among others. The key to managing mistakes in your investment life is to first assume mistakes are going to be made. Above all else, you must be on guard to identify the growing intensity of possible mistakes as quickly as possible. You should also explore numerous small investments, which can lead to small mistakes. In the end they become mistakes only if you do not learn from them. One useful technique is to maintain an investment diary discussing mistakes. If a pattern of similar mistakes emerges, then the error is in your thinking, which can almost certainly be corrected.

You might argue that avoiding mistakes is a much better solution than making them, even in limited numbers. But in many years of observation I have seen that people with a deep-seated desire to avoid making any mistakes choose not to play. "If I do not invest my money in stocks, then I will not lose any money in stocks" is their quite logical reasoning. The other side of that reasoning, however, is this: "If I do not invest my money in stocks, then I will not make any money in stocks." Given the history of stock markets, the latter argument is where the mistake actually occurs. If you do not play, you cannot win. Avoiding mistakes is a wrongheaded choice if it simultaneously means avoiding opportunity. Indeed, because inflation will probably continue in the future, today's dollars will probably purchase less in the future. You wind up losing by not playing. Worse, many people who wanted to avoid the perils of investing have found that a decline in a stock price is often merely a symptom of something else—a financial reversal at their employer or a weak economy that erodes profits and takes its toll in employment, home prices, and, eventually, higher taxes. Sometimes you just cannot escape bad fortune.

Once we acknowledge that we are going to make mistakes as the price of entry to improving our financial position, we need to differentiate between what is a mistake and what is not. Accidents, for example, need not be mistakes, at least as far as an investor is concerned. Assume you have a substantial investment in an oil-exploration company that does deep drilling in the Gulf of Mexico. Given the location of the company's operations and recent history, you should be thinking every summer and fall about the potential impact that a Category 5 hurricane can have on the investment and taking whatever steps you believe appropriate as a result. But you cannot be expected to think about the much less likely scenarios, such as an off-course and out-of-control airliner crashing into an offshore rig. Ignoring the possibility that a major hurricane could have an impact on your investment is a mistake. An airliner crashing into the rig is an accident. Both can hurt, but only one of the two scenarios should be interpreted as a mistake because only one of the two could and should reasonably have been foreseen.

One definition of a mistake, then, can be the failure to foresee something that you should have foreseen.

Changing conditions can also lead to mistakes. In my youth I spent a good deal of time at Thoroughbred racetracks. Conditions play a huge role in an individual horse's performance on the racetrack. It is an innocent or foolish bettor indeed who, after a sudden rain shower, thinks his horse in short races can come from behind. On a more sophisticated level, you can make a mistake when, after placing your bet to win at reasonably high odds, a sudden wave of money drives the odds on another horse to much lower levels and you do not at least consider that the new money knows something. At the very least you might want to bet at a different level to win or possibly diversify by betting for place (first two horses to finish) on another horse.

So another definition of a mistake is that it results in an

outcome different from what was expected because of known changing conditions.

Notice that in both types of mistakes the problem rests in a failure to recognize factors that could lead to results different from what you expected. I have seen this time and time again among investors and particularly with people of wealth, who can be very impatient. Most of their mistakes are the result of lack of analysis or thought. Carrying that observation to its logical conclusion, we can make this statement: many mistakes are our own fault. I realize that is not a welcome message. We like to be able to blame others for our misfortunes, and I often hear aggrieved investors blaming anyone but themselves. "The company lied to me," "the broker did not follow my instructions," "the seller did not disclose that the oil tank buried in the backyard was leaking." Sorry, I do not accept any of those as excuses that absolve your bruised ego from accepting some of the blame. After all, the lie was believed, the broker selected, and a less-than-complete property inspection was accepted. Just as the first step to recovery from addiction is admitting the problem, the first step toward avoiding and ameliorating mistakes is to admit that the process is your responsibility, not someone else's. That is the only way we will learn from our mistakes and diminish their future impact.

With that as background let us now think a bit about making and recognizing mistakes. There is a difference. A mistake is usually made at one point in time but not recognized until some later time as the results begin to diverge from what was expected and we try to learn why that is happening. The most common mistake one can make—and sometimes the worst—is the failure to recognize a mistake. You can neither fix nor learn from mistakes that you do not recognize. Before making an important investment of time, talent, or money, you should develop a logical outcome expectation. If a financial advisor is hired, both the investor and the advisor should have well-articulated expectations about what that advisor can and cannot accomplish. Those expectations may change over time, but they should change for reasons that both understand and acknowledge. If the hired advisor is to achieve high returns, you should have acknowledged at the outset of the relationship that those high returns may entail risks of large losses. When those losses occur, neither should be surprised. If you are truly surprised, then the initial understanding was faulty and should not be repeated.

Thoughtful analysis of your decisions and the determination of probable outcomes that will help to recognize a mistake when it occurs is not always easy. The human mind tends to focus on the accomplishment of a goal without recognizing second-, third-, and fourth-order consequences. At the track, for example, most people focus on picking the winning horse, when, in fact, the most money is made by its judicious handling. When to make small bets, when to make larger bets, and, most important, when not to bet at all are the bigger determinants of success than deciding on which horse to bet. Similarly, the biggest mistake that I see people of wealth making is a single-minded focus on investment returns with no thought about their spending patterns. At the end of the day expense control plays a larger role in the success of a financial program than the entire array of specific investments.

Once you recognize that a mistake has been made, the

recovery depends on the nature of the mistake. Some mistakes have few or no consequences. I recall an investment I made many years ago in a company that was developing a way to extend the market life of fresh fruits and vegetables through the use of nitrogen gas to delay aging while being transported. The intention was to immerse fresh-picked fruit and vegetables in nitrogen from the time the produce left the field until it was in the stores as well as in a consumer's kitchen. The business required the development and acquisition of special trucks, grocery cases, and home appliances. Unfortunately the small-scale experiments had misled the researchers. The process did not work in volume, and the early investment in trucks, grocery cases, and kitchen appliances was not productive. Yet I still made lots of money in the stock because the company that was developing the process was Whirlpool, and it was doing a great business in large home appliances. I made a mistake, but it did not cost me anything.

Other mistakes, though, can have great consequences. It is obviously best to recognize mistakes as soon as possible and correct them with the least possible damage. But as human beings we often find that hard to do. If we extract ourselves from a mistaken investment, we are, in effect, admitting our mistake and setting our losses in concrete. Many of us prefer wishful thinking as an alternative: the problem is temporary, it will be fixed, others will recognize the value of this investment and I can at least get back to my break-even point. Because we have a memory of what we paid to get into the bad investment, we somehow assume the particular investment has a memory, too. But it does not. A flipped coin that turns up heads seventeen times in a row does not remember any of those results, and the chance for a head on the next flip remains 50 percent. A security is priced at whatever its price is today because that is what someone is willing to pay for it. That it was priced twice as high last year has no relevance to the price today. As investors we must learn to acknowledge "sunken costs," the money that has already been invested and may not ever be recovered. The attempt to recover it may only result in deeper losses.

Perhaps the most important lesson we can take away from this discussion of mistakes is another that I learned at the track: mistakes are more costly in the short run than in the long run. A horse race is a form of controlled chaos, huge animals moving at amazing speed in a tightly packed group, each straining for the lead, guided by its jockey's limited and ever-changing perceptions of what is going on with the horses behind, aside, and ahead. Mistakes happen and a fast horse becomes boxed in, unable to apply its strength to gaining the lead. In a short race the finish line looms quickly and the boxed horse finishes back in the pack, much to the disappointment of all those whose bet rode alongside the jockey. In a longer race, though, the jockey and the horse have more time to escape the box and take the lead. For us as individuals, the durability of our investment performance pays in the end. Recognizing and recovering from mistakes, and changing our behavior as a consequence, helps insure that durability.

13

A LOOK IN THE MIRROR:
The Psychology of Wealth

Who are you?

The question is more complicated than you might think because I'm asking who you are as an investor, a spender, and a steward of your wealth. We all like to think of ourselves as rational decision makers, but lurking behind what we believe is rational behavior is a psychological foundation that can skew our thinking and result in less than optimum decisions. Each us is a unique blend of emotions, thoughts, intents, and behaviors that influence how we see and use wealth. I call this amalgam a person's wealth psychology. If you're willing to do the self-examination that is necessary to understand your own wealth psychology, you'll almost certainly find yourself making different—and better—decisions about wealth.

Wealth psychology manifests itself in hundreds of different ways, some obvious, some deeply hidden. On any given day you have what you think is current information—it's probably not as current as you think it is—about the state of the economy and the markets. Whether you view that information optimistically or pessimistically is a function of your wealth psychology. You may see danger approaching while someone else sees an opportunity emerging.

Consider how psychology can affect something as seemingly simple as the decision to sell a stock. Obviously when you sell that stock, a buyer is on the other side of the trade. Rarely is the individual or institution on one side considerably smarter or dumber than the one on the other side. Why have they simultaneously agreed on the same price? One possible explanation is that the buyer has a different time horizon than the seller, who wishes to exit today. But that motivation alone is seldom sufficient to explain the decision to trade. I have found that most trades are caused by some reactions to a series of data points, events, or realizations that result from each of us viewing the same information differently. The stock we decide to sell is usually a small piece of our wealth and fits into our overall scheme in different ways. What was the original purpose of the investment? What degree of satisfaction or dissatisfaction have we experienced with this specific investment? What are the consequences of selling this investment in terms of profit or loss and tax liability? What do we intend to do with the proceeds of the sale?

The answers to those questions begin to reveal the investor's psychology. Perhaps the stock has become too big a part in the portfolio and the disciplined investor wants to sell a portion of it to balance risks. Another investor could be selling when the stock returns to a break-even level at which it was purchased in a burst of unwarranted enthusiasm. That is a common symptom indicating a deep desire to avoid acknowledging a mistake and a personality devoted more to literal score-keeping than a focus on the changing dynamics of the stock market and the companies traded there.

Psychology can play an equally influential role in the decision to buy a stock. We often see buyers selecting a stock after an extended price increase, while other investors shun the same stock as overpriced. The buyers often see the price rise as proof that others value the stock. That is particularly true when a well-known investor has been reported to be buying the stock. When the investment works, this technique is called affinity investing. When it does not, it gets labeled crony capitalism.

Some of the components of your wealth psychology may seem easily discerned. Age is the most obvious example. Typically, someone who is twenty-five years old may view and use wealth differently from someone sixty-five years old. That is not to say that every twenty-five-year-old has the same wealth psychology as every other twenty-five-year-old, only that youth and maturity provide different perspectives. Being older is not necessarily a reason to be more conservative. I recall one client who was well into her nineties when she came to us with instructions to invest a considerable sum in funds that invest in small-company growth stocks. Doing our due diligence, we asked why she wanted to pursue that particular theme, and she said, "Look, if the market drops, then I'm passing on to my heirs stocks with low valuations and lots of room to grow. If I die when the market is up, then they're getting a portfolio of very valuable stocks and it's better for them to sell than for me to sell because their tax basis is the price the day I die." Clearly she had applied her future-oriented psychology to optimize her heirs' wealth, not her own.

The sources of wealth also have a powerful influence on our wealth psychology. A person who inherits wealth will think about that wealth differently from a person who has taken a big risk and worked long and hard to create wealth as a founder of a company. Again, that is not to say that everyone who inherits a fortune will be affected by or use it the same way, only that the fact of inheritance will have some effect on the perception of wealth.

Other aspects of wealth psychology are less obvious. A common perception among people who do not possess wealth is that having a fortune provides security. Wealth certainly can. But it can also create anxiety and stress if you worry about losing that wealth, obsess over managing it, or let it become a distraction that prevents you from focusing on things that may be more important to you, such as career and family.

Wealth psychology can have a darker side. With wealth comes perceived power. Whether consciously or unconsciously people can attempt to use wealth to control, reward, or punish others, as well as themselves. Such uses of wealth are often manifested in relationships with employees or advisors as well as heirs.

Things get more complicated when you consider that you are not alone with either your wealth or your wealth psychology. In almost every case others are interested—sometimes vitally so— in the wealth you have, and you sometimes have to take into account their wealth psychology and how it matches or diverges from yours. Even the simple act of discussing your wealth, whether with your lawyer or accountant or with your spouse and children, is fraught with potential psychological problems. I know for certain that only a few wealthy people tell their lawyers the same thing they tell their tax accountants. They probably do not mean to withhold important information from a key advisor, but they think of people on the basis of what they were originally hired to do. Lawyers are used to protect against known and unknown liabilities, including some of the unspecified liabilities to yourself and others. Most people employ their personal accountant to deal only with tax matters, unfortunately, not overall financial management.

Even when discussing financial affairs with your spouse or children, it is not a simple matter of sitting down around the dinner table for a heart-to-heart discussion. First, the discussion has to take place in terms that everyone understands. Can you, if required, explain sometimes complex financial concepts clearly? More important, though, is your evaluation of the people to whom you want to convey this information. Are they all equally interested in the welfare of the family as a unit, or are some likely to be focused on "What's in it for me?" Your own self-confidence may be put to the test if someone disagrees with your intentions or methods. One major reason that you might not wish to have such a discussion is that it can convince some heirs that they now "own" a particular asset. Over time, conditions change, both in your total portfolio and in the lives and conditions of potential heirs. You may find a sound reason to decrease the amount to be passed to one or more heirs. The "losers" may feel that you suddenly love them less and fail to see that in your mind someone else needs more. A related issue is the claim that often arises at the end of life that someone among the heirs is exercising improper influence that has caused the will and the trusts to be changed. If heirs did not know the original wishes, they will not have a road map to the changes.

Neither this nor any other book is likely to have much effect on some of the more deeply rooted emotions and behaviors that are part of your own wealth psychology. But you can take a practical approach to wealth psychology that may help you recognize some of the traits and biases that influence, for better or worse, how you view and use your wealth. Something as seemingly simple as choosing the right financial advisors can be derailed by certain psychological traits. More seriously, unwarranted fears or equally unwarranted confidence can lead to investments that fail to deliver the needed performance to meet important goals. In the next few chapters I'll examine more intensely some of the causes and effects of wealth psychology.

14

INVESTOR, KNOW THYSELF:
The Ten Investment Personalities

We are all individuals and bring to our investments a myriad of quirks, eccentricities, presumptions, and assumptions. I think it is fair to say that no two individuals think about and pursue their investment strategies and goals in exactly the same ways. Yet amid that incredible variety I have over the years identified what I think are some personality types that tend to cover almost all the investors I have known. These types are by no means mutually exclusive. Some investors manifest all ten personality types simultaneously, although one is usually dominant! And the personality types can change over time to the extent that if you were to lose track of an investor friend and then meet that person one day twenty years later, you would be flabbergasted to find that your friend's approach to investing has changed 180 degrees from when you last saw him. Each of the ten investor personalities that I have identified has its strengths and weaknesses. By thinking a bit about which one of the following personalities most closely reflects your own approach to investing and wealth management, you can make an extra effort to take further advantage of your strengths while simultaneously taking steps to avoid the mistakes inherent in your view of finances.

THE ABSOLUTE INVESTOR

The absolute investor tends to have a strong personality and to be highly certain about the capital he has available and the return he needs to get, even if that return includes invading the capital to keep a predetermined level of income flowing. This need for certainty often drives the absolute investor into high-quality bonds. And because the financial needs often extend to another generation, the bonds that make up much of the portfolio tend to be of lengthy maturities. While U.S. Treasury bonds can be purchased that mature thirty years hence, that often isn't sufficiently long for the absolute investor, who may seek longer-term bonds issued by other sovereign governments. Insurance products may also provide some of that certainty over long periods of time. Unless they have sufficient assets to assure a lifelong flow of income at whatever levels they feel they need, absolute investors should recognize the threat that inflation poses for their investment portfolios and thus place at least some of their investments in equities. But not just any stock or mutual fund will do. They prefer stocks that are paying a reasonably assured and hopefully growing dividend, but the stocks should not be high-yielding issues since the high yields are often indicative of above-average risk both in terms of price and the sustainability of current dividends.

Yet for all their self-assured certainty, these absolute investors tend to produce subpar performance. One of their biggest failings is the lack of full recognition of the effects of inflation and taxes. Long-term bonds can certainly be useful instruments, but the certainty of the return makes it lower than that of other, riskier investments. I know at least a few of these absolute investors who quickly seized on a variety of very long-term bonds issued in the early 1990s—Walt Disney Co. issued a hundred-year bond and Boeing, Texaco, Conrail, and the Tennessee Valley Authority issued fifty-year bonds—to lock in assured long-term rates. Of course, the treasurers of those companies were smart people who were locking in low interest rates that they calculated were a bargain. Insurance products, an alternative to long-term bonds, have their own problems. Even when they are issued by strong insurance companies with solid credit ratings and even some backup from state-mandated insurance-industry contingency funds, there is some risk to full and timely payment. And, as with the long-term bonds, the payments made by those insurance products tend to be low. Finally, while the best of the dividend-paying stocks are inherently good investments, companies that reinvest their profits into intelligent expansion tend to have better stock performance. Unless an investor has a clear understanding of the underlying business, a dividend-paying stock can be saddled with deteriorating fundamentals that can result in a cessation of dividends and even bankruptcy.

My own view is that the world is changing too much and too fast for anyone to seek the certainty of an absolute return. A level of certainty can be achieved for short periods, and, in some cases, for longer periods, but almost always at the cost of higher, albeit more volatile, returns elsewhere.

THE CONFIDENT INVESTOR

The confident investor is very different from the absolute investor in that he or she doesn't seek a specific return, but chases instead the "best" return. As the term implies, the confident investor harbors few or any doubts about his investment skills. This person believes in bold moves and often organizes his portfolio with only a limited number of holdings in stocks, bonds, and funds. After all, most of them will be winners! Investment selections are usually based on the recent short-term performance of the investments. The emphasis tends to be more on growth stocks of companies with rising earnings rather than on value stocks, the "value" of which may not be realized for some time. These investors usually hold on to their investments until their expectations of rising prices are realized. And what if they aren't and the investor winds up selling at a loss? The losses are almost invariably someone else's fault, because of lies the company told or faulty advice from an advisor. Bonds have little role in a confident investor's portfolio and are most often used either to dampen the volatility of a portfolio or to serve as a ready reserve of funds to take advantage of the next big stock opportunity that comes along.

The great advantage that the confident investor has over the rest of us is that he doesn't have to spend a lot of time worrying about his portfolio. The great disadvantage that the confident investor suffers from is that he does not spend a lot of time worrying about his portfolio. He is immune to new information or market inputs that may significantly undermine his basic investment assumptions. Consequently he winds up more frequently in need of someone else to blame for losses or at least lackluster performance among his investments. And because those investments are highly concentrated, unhedged, and focused on growth rather than value stocks, the performance is volatile and, more often than not, less than what could be obtained from a more balanced and diversified approach to investing.

THE UNCERTAIN INVESTOR

Surprising as it may seem, I deem the uncertain investor to be the most intelligent among the various investment personalities. The reason is simple: investing is uncertain, and the uncertain investor is the only one among the types who recognizes that and adapts to it. This person knows that things can and do go wrong. Sometimes those things can be identified and defended against, while at other times they come as a complete surprise. Despite being burdened by both the known unknowns as well as the unknown unknowns, the uncertain investor courageously invests because he knows he must. He is aware of a cardinal rule of investing: not to invest is to make an investment decision. Among the uncertainties that weigh on these seemingly hapless but actually savvy investors is the inability to define the future as well as the lack of clarity about the uses of his capital and the timing of various spending requirements. Thus this person tends to have a widely diversified portfolio, including bonds in a wide range of maturities. The uncertain investor tends to prefer value stocks, realizing that the fundamental backbone of value investing is the search for mispriced securities and a belief that some mechanism will eventually reveal the correct, higher value. The uncertainty is what that mechanism is and when it will emerge. This kind of investing requires patience. Given his uncertainties, this investor maintains a tactical reserve of cash that can quickly be deployed to buy bargains or used to cushion some future decline in the market. Fortunately, most investors, most of the times, are uncertain investors.

The problems confronting uncertain investors occur when their sensitivity meter is turned up too high and they become not just uncertain, but nervous. Under those conditions the uncertain investor tends to trade faster and more frequently. Almost any fragment of news is interpreted as a call to action. This high-frequency trading results in higher expenses and taxes and often leaves the uncertain investor whipsawed by the normal volatility of markets.

THE RELATIVE INVESTOR

The relative investor is a good scorekeeper. He or she is obsessed with measuring the performance of his or her portfolio against that of some benchmark. His fondest desire is to realize a better return than a benchmark's. This investor treats his portfolio as if it's part of some athletic contest. He wants to know which side is winning—his portfolio or the benchmark—and by how much. And, as with much sports commentary, little information is sought about the quality of whatever result is on the scoreboard, that is, whether the result was hard fought or easy or if the nature of the opposition changed midway through the game. For many years in the United States the standard benchmark against which relative investors scored themselves was the Dow Jones Industrial Average. More recently the Standard & Poor's 500 Stock Index has become the benchmark of choice, although others, in different circumstances, have more utility, including the Value Line, Russell, Wilshire, and MSCI measures of the market. Broadly speaking, relative investors tend to pursue one of two strategies in their effort to best a benchmark: first, selecting investments that are not contained in the benchmark, such as smaller-capitalization or foreign stocks, or second, confining the selection of equities to only those within the benchmark that are most likely to perform well. That leaves the benchmark to be held back by its laggard components.

While I recognize that our performance-oriented culture wants to measure relative success or failure and does it constantly in many parts of our lives, I find the relative investor is fooling himself. If, for example, he tries to "win" against a benchmark by investing in stocks that aren't part of the benchmark, the question immediately arises of how appropriate is the chosen benchmark under such circumstances. More to the point, however, is that the relative investor, even if he confines himself to stocks held within the benchmark or at least to stocks with similar characteristics, seldom understands why he wins or loses against the benchmark. As someone who learned analysis at the racetrack, I long ago learned that the crucial elements of a given race take place long before the gates swing open: how the horse spent the night in his stall, how the morning workouts went, how the jockey matches the mount and knows the competition (with alternative plans to run the race depending upon which horse emerges as the primary challenger), and, finally, the conditions of the track. The one thing that doesn't matter is what everyone at the track watches: the changing odds on the tote board. The lesson of both the track and the Street is that the crowd rarely wins big and mostly suffers small losses. The relative investor would be better off to take a more analytical approach to his performance, measuring similar stocks or funds against one another and measuring their performance over various periods to understand not just how his investment performed, but why it performed the way it did.

THE FIDUCIARY INVESTOR

The fiduciary investor feels a responsibility to the future users of the capital he or she is currently investing. This definition of a "fiduciary" investor is different from the legal term that obligates an advisor to act in the best interests of the client, but the long-term effect is essentially the same. Many fiduciary investors have become wealthy as the result of their own hard work, but recognize that their talents alone were not enough to get them to where they are today. Circumstances had to be right and they had to recognize opportunities when they arose. They realize that others around them may be equally smart and ambitious but may not catch the right breaks to generate their own wealth. These investors feel grateful and desire to "give back" something to people or charities. The task of the fiduciary investor is to allocate and invest funds in different ways to meet the differing needs of the recipients of the benefits. Typically, for instance, some beneficiaries receive income from investments and other beneficiaries will eventually receive the principal or capital. Juggling the two is more of an art than a science, made somewhat simpler when the fiduciary investor seeks a total return that provides both income and capital appreciation. These investors tend to focus on high-quality investments to avoid criticism, but that approach sometimes generates criticism, particularly during the manic phase of a speculative market when riskier investments are producing far higher returns. You cannot satisfy everybody all the time.

STAR PERFORMERS

This psychological type is often but not exclusively found in show business and professional sports, arenas in which stars are paid huge salaries or fees, often at a relatively young age. What differentiates this type from other wealthy people is that they often seek or at least become accustomed to the adulation of throngs of people. If that need for adulation penetrates their psyche too deeply, they become unable to make sound long-term decisions about their financial lives and the people who will manage their finances. Rather than finding objective, skilled advisors, they tend to look for supplicants and sycophants. Poor advice coupled with self-indulgence and the need to make an impression on fans can easily result in the loss of a fortune as careers, often dependent upon physical abilities and appearances, wane over time.

I do not know Michael Jackson, but judging by what I've read over the years he's the archetype of the star performer. Clearly Jackson is immensely talented, and he became fabulously wealthy as a child. His talent was such that he carried it well into adulthood. His *Thriller* album sold 51 million copies and still stands as the bestselling album of all time. He was as close as one gets to becoming a moneymaking machine. He may also be a much smarter investor than many think. After all, he had the savvy to purchase a controlling interest in the Beatles' library of songs, an asset worth an estimated $1 billion today. But Jackson apparently had little self-control. Lavish spending on himself and his friends and advisors has already caused defaults on some loans, and he has had to defend himself against some suits alleging failure to pay obligations. Where his money managers were and what they were advising is not clear. Either Jackson had bad advice, perhaps from managers so eager to keep their relationship with him that they did not confront his disastrous spending, or he ignored good advice. In any event, he may have come perilously close to squandering his immense fortune.

Both athletes and actors depend heavily on their various advisors. Those advisors doubtless have well-developed skills, such as publicizing their clients or making contacts with other important or useful people, but foremost among them is the ability to maintain relationships with their clients as well as with those who pay their clients. With the exception of wealth advisors, those skills generally do not extend to investments, taxes, or estates. That does not always stop them, however, from offering advice in those areas or from proposing to their clients who should become advisors in such matters. In the institutional investing world, such people are called gatekeepers. Good gatekeepers serve an important screening function by keeping inappropriate or unskilled advisors out of the client's way. They should not, however, prevent skilled advisors who may have a different point of view from the client's from discussing that view. That is why, I suspect, so many stars wind up putting their hard-earned cash into developing high-profile restaurants—notoriously difficult and unforgiving businesses—instead of well-diversified stock and bond portfolios.

Star performers must develop three essential ingredients if they are to succeed financially. The first is the realization that their career is tenuous. National Football League players have an average playing career of three seasons. Entertainers with abundant talent can endure for a lifetime, but if beauty rather than talent is the primary asset, the career passes into old age long before the person. The second is the ability to say no. Star performers will almost always find that they have a large number of "friends"—former schoolmates, long-lost relatives, and friends of friends—all of whom know how to spend or invest the star's money better than the star does. Finally, they need to understand and be comfortable with the concept of diversification. Many follow the easy route and invest in what is familiar—a production company or a sports team—but they already have too much invested in show business or sports in the form of those risky careers.

THE BORED INVESTOR

The bored investor is most likely to have inherited wealth that was created two or three generations earlier. I find the bored investor to be akin to bored spectators at sports events: they know the score, but they don't really understand how the game evolved or the various strategies and tactics that each team employed, either successfully or unsuccessfully, or even the names of the players or where to find the names of the officials. Many bored investors use their apparent lack of interest in their investments as a disguise that conceals a deep insecurity about financial matters. They prefer to spend little time monitoring their investments or discussing investment strategies with advisors. Typically they sign their tax returns without reviewing them, content to take the word of their accountant that all is in order. They look to their financial advisors for only the most basic information: how much can I spend, how rich am I, and how long will my capital last? They own securities for the income stream they provide, not to build wealth for future generations or for charitable purposes. They want a portfolio that is comfortable, that contains names of companies they easily recognize. Thus their stock holdings tend to perform in parallel with the blue chips of the Dow Jones Industrial Average. Their bond holdings are high-quality issues from known companies or government entities, and they shy away from bond funds because of the uncertainty of returns. When the bored investor hires a financial advisor, it is usually one of the best-known in the community, a firm or individual who will, if the account is large enough, invite the bored one to an annual lunch at which the topic of finances arises only superficially.

I've found it difficult to get bored investors to take an interest in their finances. Their lack of interest is not limited to finances. Often they display an alarming lack of interest in anything else, including politics, sports, or their communities. Simply put, they have no passion. Fortunately, the bored investor's tendencies toward the large and familiar produce a reasonably stable return over time, although without a focus on long-term growth. The best thing that can happen to a bored investor is to have a potential personal or charitable heir take an interest in the account and reconnect the bored one with his or her money and the responsibilities they have to themselves and to their heirs.

THE GUILTY INVESTOR

This personality type is one of the most puzzling. The guilty investor seems to feel that he doesn't deserve his good fortune, and the money becomes a curse on life rather than a source of happiness or satisfaction. Many of the guilt-ridden investors are bright and accomplished in their own fields, but they seem to turn off their rational thinking when it comes to investing. This is one reason that so many bright people tend to be poor investors. I strongly suspect some guilty investors may be cheating, perhaps on their spouse (or significant other), their taxes, or their business partner. Others take a dim view of the source of their wealth if it was created by previous generations engaged in what the guilty investor considers unsavory commerce or a bad marriage. Few have a deep or abiding concern for heirs, either personal or charitable, and seem to prefer to lose their money through bad investments than to give it away. I know it's difficult to conceive of such people, but they're certainly out there. Often the evidence of a guilty investor is a long, long string of bad investment decisions resulting in steady losses. We all suffer an occasional bout of bad luck, but luck comes in streaks that reverse. The guilty investor's losing streak never seems to reverse itself. More evidence comes from the nature of the investments themselves: junk bonds, volatile stocks, and highly speculative schemes of various sorts. The irony of this approach is that some of those investments could by accident pay off handsomely.

In truth many guilty investors would benefit from psychological, not financial, counseling. Absent such help, financial advisors working with a guilty investor are best advised to try to introduce the client to the concept of stewardship, using wealth for the benefit of others. If the guilty investor accepts a responsibility to use his wealth for others, he can be persuaded to abandon his dangerous approach to investing in favor of a more conservative and balanced strategy that will benefit him and his heirs.

THE FINANCIAL DEATH-WISH INVESTOR

This is a variant on some of the other personality types, distinguished from them in that the investor is often someone who is highly successful and capable in a chosen profession, but cannot apply the same effort and intellect to investing that has led to the investor's success in another area. In their own sphere of interest, they are intensely focused and detail-oriented. They are skeptical about new developments in their field, they think about the subject constantly, and they are inundated with publications related to their field. Most important, they are willing to acknowledge to themselves when something is not working and reverse course, extricating themselves and learning something from the mistake. Because of their success, they have generated some degree of wealth, often through patented products or specialized services. But ask them to look after their wealth and to insure that it is either growing or being preserved, and they become helpless, listless, and uninterested. They have no conception of an overall wealth strategy, they have no interest in reading about the subject or watching the markets, and they do not have a sense of how well their investments are performing. If and when they take a brief interest in investing, they seem intent on making the kinds of investments that a rational person would argue have high odds of failure. But more likely, they establish spending patterns that will over time eventually reduce their assets to little or nothing. Unfortunately, people with this financial death wish are not amenable to help. They do not realize what they are doing, do not care if told, and will often make poor choices among financial advisors if prompted by relatives or friends to seek financial help. They are among the saddest cases I have seen over my career.

THE PARALYTIC INVESTOR

To call this type an "investor" is incorrect since they do little investing. Superficially they appear somewhat similar to the financial death-wish investor. Observing them for a short time, one might conclude that this kind of investor is either neglectful or lazy, or some combination of the two. Essentially nothing happens. Money from salary, inheritance, or other sources builds up over time in a bank checking account or, if they have bestirred themselves minimally, in a money-market fund. I think that something more subtle is going on with them related to a feeling of inferiority that stems from a false set of comparisons. Perhaps they believe initially that they are not as "good" as their brother or sister at some undertaking such as education. They then extend that feeling of inadequacy into all other aspects of their life, including investing. Given their self-perception that they are not good, they are unwilling to make decisions. They realize intellectually that this paralysis will harm their investment returns, yet they have concluded that it is better to make no decision than to make a decision that then goes wrong. Of course we all know that not making a decision is, in effect, making a decision. Unlike the financial death-wish investor, these people are amenable to help, but only if an advisor has the insight and patience to focus on the real problem, not just the financial instruments he may have to offer them. The good thing about this personality type is that he or she seldom develops a destructive spending pattern. The result is that their wealth grows slowly. They are the closest modern equivalent I can think of to the elderly who stuffed their money under their mattresses as a consequence of the horrors of the Great Depression.

15

COMING TO GRIPS
WITH MORTALITY:
Wills, Trusts, and Heirs

O ne of the most powerful documents that most people sign is their last will and testament. Especially among the wealthy a will has immense power to do great good or to wreak havoc and emotional turmoil. Not surprisingly, I think the drafting of a will should be a serious undertaking, one to which you devote considerable thought. Yet most people, particularly those of wealth, go about creating their will backward. The first and sometimes only person they talk to about their will is a lawyer. There's no question that a good trusts and estates attorney can convert your words into language that will give your heirs and, if necessary, the probate court a clear understanding on how your executors or personal representative should dispose of your assets. From his experience and the study of various cases the attorney should be able to produce an unambiguous document. He may also have some ideas about the drafting of the document that may reduce the tax impact on the estate and heirs. These services are of value, but they are most effectively used after you have decided how you want to dispose of your worldly goods.

The discussion with the trusts and estates lawyer should come later because most people have not seriously pondered and come to grips with the certainty of their demise and the possibility of mental and emotional incapacitation. As with many important issues the questions are easy to ask, the answers often difficult to obtain. The central question is relatively simple: what do you want your heirs, both individual and charitable, to do with your assets in terms of accomplishing some goals? For the first and perhaps the last time you must think about the goals that your heirs are pursuing now and are likely to pursue in the future. While you may believe that you have some control of their present actions and goals, your ability to "command" their behavior after you are gone is limited and may well be self-defeating. Ruling through the dead hand from the grave has never been effective in the long run. You, perhaps with the assistance of someone trained in the process, should determine the likely results of passing hard assets to your heirs.

The reason lawyers refer to a "trust and estate" practice is that many wills are designed to pass assets out of the will and into trusts. In addition, for tax and other reasons trusts can and should be used before death. While these are the proper province of a skilled T&E lawyer, his work should be coordinated with a tax accountant who is knowledgeable about these matters. Careful draftsmanship can save significantly on income and estate taxes. Viewing things from the investment advisor's vantage point, most of the long-term success in shifting assets to the use of heirs is a function of how the hard assets are invested before and after death. Currently, assets are stepped up to the date-of-death valuation, without paying taxes on the unrealized gains. For this reason many wealthy people with substantial unrealized gains are reluctant to sell and will either let the estate sell or pass on the appreciated assets to the heirs. This investment decision should be reviewed with an investment professional. A personal example may be illustrative. By chance, I am the owner of a few shares of Apple Computer with a tax cost of sixteen cents while the stock sells for over $100. Unless there are changes in the law and taxes, my guess is that those shares will be in my estate and then be sold by a charity or another heir. If, on the other hand, those shares were in some respect control shares of a company, those shares would probably be transferred to someone who could make a good decision for the family largely regardless of the investment merits.

Since many estates take some time to be settled and trusts set up, I have concluded that an important part of my assets will be invested in active and to a lesser-degree passive funds. Once the assets finally come to rest in their more permanent position, other investment approaches could be appropriate if capable investment people are available to make decisions.

I suggest that once you reach Social Security retirement age (59½ to 70½), you should begin devoting some careful attention to the possible disposition of investment assets at each periodic review of the investment portfolio. At the same time you should retain an investment advisor to help grow and care for the assets. And to be on the safe side, you might also begin looking for someone who can help your heirs sort out their own financial situations. To put some number on the size of the problem, a relatively recent telephone survey by Harris Interactive (another accidental holding of mine) found that of 1,018 people surveyed more than half did not have a will. Many of us may have had a will drawn up when we got married or had our first child, but these are now badly out-of-date in light of our assets and attitudes toward potential heirs, including charities. Further, I would suggest that at the minimum your will and trusts should be reviewed at least every five years or sooner if circumstances warrant. For this review a meeting with your lawyer, accountant, and investment advisor would raise the kinds of questions you should deal with if you are going to be an effective steward of your assets.

While discussions of wills and trusts tend to center around the estate's hard assets—cash, stocks, bonds, real estate—I have long believed that your "soft" assets are, in the long run, of greater value to your heirs. Your reputation for dealing with others with integrity and good humor as well as the extensive nature of your contacts can be of great help to your heirs. To some extent you can let your heirs use these assets to their own benefit during your lifetime. I also believe—and not everyone will agree with this viewpoint—that we do not own anything! After we are gone, our assets will be used by others, be they our personal, charitable, or, in some cases, corporate heirs. While we may try to control their actions from the grave, our instructions are not likely to be fully and forever completely obeyed. Worse, because of changing conditions, personalities, laws, and taxes our instructions may well become counterproductive to our original intent. When you think about it, you may well realize the various hard assets that we are so proud of accumulating were in some-one else's hands before they came under our own control. In effect, we are either renters of assets or, more charitably, stew-ards of the assets for others who will follow us. Thus in planning to dispose of your assets you need to contemplate what would be the best way for your heirs to understand that you deeply cared about them and to the extent possible want to help them accom-plish their critical missions. In deciding on the ways you want to help, you will also have to decide what is the likelihood of your heirs being able and willing to make what you believe to be the correct investment and other decisions.

In practical terms you should consider each heir's individ-ual needs. An heir, be it an individual or a charity, who does not need current income may have long-term capital needs. Such an account should be targeted for optimum capital growth while being able to tolerate periodic declines in value. This future-oriented account should be invested with man-agers who have a keen sense of what new products and serv-ices are hidden beyond the typical investor's view. The use of these new opportunities should not be limited by restrictions on market capitalization. These opportunities are often found in smaller-market-capitalization stocks that trade in the United States or beyond. But some can also be found in larger compa-nies. Thus it is unwise to invest only with small-cap managers or funds. One hopes these investment opportunities will gener-ate large gains, but it must be understood that they may also produce large losses.

If the potential for dramatic ups and downs is too much for other beneficiaries to stomach, then you must turn to a manager or a fund that is more price-disciplined. Such a manager or fund can be expected to produce good results and may, depending upon market conditions, produce better results than a highly focused "growth-oriented' manager may produce. Often these are called "value" managers or funds. They seek to buy assets that they consider "undervalued" when compared to their estimates of what a knowledgeable financial buyer might pay for the company with the idea of liquidating it. The financial buyer may, for example, perceive more financial-leverage or dividend-production capacity than the current managers are using. Another approach is to estimate the price that a strategic buyer would pay to operate the business or merge it into another company. These values are more difficult to determine, but generally rest on the assumption that more operating leverage is available to the acquirer than the current operator is displaying.

Other beneficiary needs are purely income-driven. That sounds as if it would be a relatively easy need to fulfill, but the recent malaise that affected the subprime mortgage market and that spread both globally and to higher-quality investments tells us that fixed income can be both dangerous and produce uncertain returns. I would therefore rank fixed-income instruments based upon the following attributes:

Tax preference (taxable, tax-exempt, AMT, state/city)

Income before or after inflation

Current income (or total return to encompass price movement)

Variability of income (by month, quarter, and due to maturities)

Quality of issuers and covenants (critical in corporate bonds
and theoretically important among government agencies
and treasuries)

Many managers and funds believe that they can and must attempt to add value over the stated interest rate by trading. While
I have a bias against investing for income, many accounts need
it, and some managers can produce it.

No manager or fund is perfect for all times. Thus the wealthy
can and should have more than one provider for each need; that
is, two funds doing essentially the same things with the same
portfolios. While the funds will have similar objectives, they will
probably go about accomplishing their missions differently.

While in the ideal world there should be a separate account
or fund for each need, it will seldom work out so neatly. Either
the capital or, more likely, the patience of the investor will be in
short supply. In that case, three other investment vehicles can
do an adequate but not optimum job. The first of the three are
balanced funds, the oldest type of portfolio created by trust and
estate lawyers. By varying the mix of assets between stocks and
bonds, both the income beneficiary and the capital beneficiary
(often called the remainder man) can reasonably well be served.
This arrangement may not produce optimum financial results,
but can keep peace within the family. The second trade-off vehicle, which for many years was the most popular mutual-fund
type and the policy followed by most trust departments, is the
growth and income fund. While some of these funds may have
some fixed-income issues in their portfolios, the bulk of their income comes from dividends from reasonably mature companies.

In a down market, the combination of the income generated and the maturity of the companies often produces a less volatile return compared to the more growth-focused funds. The trade-off is their lag in a rapidly expanding market. The third trade-off vehicle and the most modern is the index fund. In the 1930s, a number of these passively invested in a list of well-known stocks. The modern version started by duplicating the portfolio of the Standard & Poor's 500. The trade-off in index funds is that they provide close to a "market" return, but forgo the possibility of beating the market and fail to recognize that market dynamics are constantly changing. Today, over four hundred Exchange Traded Funds (ETFs) are built on various indexes and can be used along with open-end index funds to provide cover for those who wish to demonstrate close to "market" performance at the next cocktail party.

PART TWO

APPROACHES
TO INVESTING

16

CREATING AN INVESTMENT COLOSSUS:
The Lessons of Magellan

Some wealthy people would not think about owning a mutual fund. They have various financial and legal advisors to manage their money for them with a much greater degree of control than that offered by a mutual fund. Yet I believe that a close look at the history of Fidelity's Magellan Fund offers some worthwhile lessons for anyone interested in financial stewardship. Magellan became the world's best-known mutual fund not just because of the investment savvy of the various managers who have run it over the past four decades, but also because of governance policies—some good, some bad—and the creation and destruction of various investment philosophies over the years. Those same factors can—indeed, almost certainly will— recur in the future and have major effects, some good and some bad, on our own wealth and that of our heirs.

In America, names can mean everything or nothing. Some of

the early families that came to the United States take deep pride in their family name, the Lodges, Astors, and Carnegies, for example. But many of our forebears either chose to anglicize their names or had them anglicized by careless or impatient immigration officials. Mutual funds and the companies that run them aren't much different. Fund names change over time, but they tend to hew to one of three naming conventions: the owners' corporate or individual name (Oppenheimer Funds), the location of the fund's headquarters (Congress Street Funds or 59 Wall Street Funds), or the fund's investment focus (Vanguard Growth and Income Fund).

What we know today as the Fidelity Magellan Fund began life with the filing of a prospectus on December 31, 1962, for a mutual fund to be called the Fidelity International Fund, a name that reflected its corporate ownership and its investment focus. The name suggested that the fund would invest in companies without regard to their national domicile. The fund was formally offered for sale on May 2, 1963, but to a limited audience: sales were nominally restricted to residents of the state of Massachusetts and in reality to Fidelity insiders and their friends.

Yet even before it began to accumulate any performance record the fund was forced to change its strategy. In 1963 interest rates in Europe were considerably higher than interest rates in the United States. Not surprisingly those higher rates lured U.S. dollars to Europe. In a particularly shortsighted move, the Congress approved and President Lyndon B. Johnson imposed the Interest Equalization Tax that effectively penalized any U.S. investors who bought foreign securities. The impact was immediate and painful. First, U.S. investors stopped investing abroad and lost the valuable benefits of international selection. Second, and most important, the United States lost control of all those dollars that were already outside its borders. Given the large number of dollars already abroad and the near-term prospect that no more would be coming from the United States, some savvy financiers saw an opportunity. Ironically, it was the London office of the Moscow-Narodney Bank, controlled by Communists in Moscow, that first recognized the opportunity and formed a new market for the so-called Eurodollars. The Eurodollar market became a major source of funding, especially of debt instruments that carried a different interest rate than had the dollars been borrowed directly from U.S. institutions. The Eurodollar became the first stateless currency accepted worldwide in financial circles and, in fact, was the precursor for today's euro.

More germane to our story, however, is that the imposition of the Interest Equalization Tax put the Fidelity International Fund in a difficult position since its mandate was to roam the world buying stocks. As a result of the tax Fidelity restructured its prospectus to focus on stocks that could be bought in the United States but that had an international bent. The first portfolio of the renamed Magellan Fund that I have seen was in the April 22, 1965, prospectus. It showed the fund holding twenty-eight stocks with a market value of $423,763 and a cost of $364,556. The stocks it held clearly reflected its continuing focus on companies with international operations. It owned Hilton International and TransWorld Airlines, both of which, although U.S. companies, had substantial international presences. It also owned KLM Royal Dutch Airlines, which was domiciled in the Netherlands but whose stock also traded in New York.

More interesting, though, were some of the domestic stock-holdings, which included Admiral Corp. (television sets), National Video (television picture tubes), and Solitron Devices (electronics). Granted, that was a time of major expansion for consumer electronics, but the more interesting aspect of those three holdings is that they were all highly operationally leveraged. That meant that even relatively small gains in sales could sharply raise earnings. The reverse was true, as well—a small reduction in sales could sharply lower earnings. The stock prices of such leveraged companies were considerably more volatile than those of less leveraged competitors. In other words, as each new bit of information came in that showed whether leverage was working for or against one of these companies, the stock price would quickly adjust. Timing and trading execution were critical to maximizing the benefits of such a portfolio, and Fidelity excelled at both. Indeed, the turnover among Fidelity funds' holdings was so high during that period that some wags began calling it the In-fidelity Group.

An investment manager's portfolio and trading patterns are an important part of reaching a judgment about the manager. But so, too, is the ownership structure of his firm. The 1965 prospectus reveals some clues about how Fidelity and Magellan would develop over the coming years. First, the advisor for the Magellan Fund was identified as Fidelity Management & Research, a name purposely chosen to reflect a focus on research as a guide to stock picking. The prospectus also revealed two classes of ownership stock—voting and nonvoting. Edward C. Johnson II, known universally in the investment community as Mr. Johnson, owned 68 percent of the voting stock and 32 percent of the nonvoting stock. His son Edward C. Johnson III (whom I and everyone else who has known him call Ned) owned 22 percent of the voting stock and 23.1 percent of the nonvoting stock. Gerald Tsai, a brilliant and dynamic stock picker who had joined the firm in 1952, owned 19.1 percent of the nonvoting stock. The rest was held by a variety of trusted employees and by one institutional investor.

Gerry Tsai and Ned Johnson were both named directors of Fidelity in 1961. To some observers it looked like a classic horse race for the leadership of Fidelity. Mr. Johnson had hired Tsai, a young immigrant from Shanghai, as a stock analyst and in 1957 turned over the Fidelity Capital Fund to him. Ned Johnson was put in charge of the Fidelity Trend Fund in 1961, and the competition began! Tsai made his name buying speculative stocks such as Xerox and Polaroid. His ebullient personality made him a darling of the media. Ned, on the other hand, was shy and reserved but had a penetrating curiosity that led him to an eclectic collection of stocks that ultimately slightly outperformed Tsai's picks. Gerry Tsai may have thought himself in the running for Mr. Johnson's job, but probably wasn't particularly surprised when Ned was given the post. Tsai left shortly thereafter and had a career marked by spectacular successes and some losses.

Ned Johnson succeeded Mr. Johnson as president of Fidelity in 1972, just as the stock market was beginning to sink into a decade-long period of poor performance. Over time Mr. Johnson ceded to Ned more and more of the voting stock until the son owned more than half of it and thus had unfettered control of the company. He maintained this absolute control for years until he reduced his position to 49 percent, apparently for tax purposes. Later he followed in his father's footsteps, passing on to his daughter, Abby, the largest single position of the voting stock, 25 percent.

Despite his later rise in the Fidelity organization Ned remains central to our story about Magellan because he was the fund's first manager. And what a manager he turned out to be! In the nine years he directed the Magellan Fund, Ned had two years of spectacular gains, 121.30 percent in 1965 and 104.95 percent in 1967. He also had two losing years—down 15.31 percent in 1969 and 15.75 percent in 1970.

When Ned succeeded Mr. Johnson in 1972 as president of the management company, Richard Haberman became the portfolio manager of the Magellan Fund. Over a tough six-year period when the stock market was in eclipse, Dick produced four up years and two down years, including the fund's single worst annual decline, of 42.18 percent in 1973. By the end of May 1977, the Magellan Fund had been operating for fifteen years and had beaten the market roughly two-thirds of the time. Still, it had only $22 million in assets, in part because it simply hadn't been marketed aggressively. The high inflation of that period prompted investors to focus more on the high interest rates offered by money-market funds, a focus that Fidelity and other fund companies were happy to accommodate.

Then Peter Lynch assumed control of the fund. Over the next thirteen years Magellan gained over 2,000 percent and its assets climbed to over $12 billion. People still debate what magic Peter Lynch brought to Magellan to propel it to such lofty heights. The truth is he was simply a product of the Fidelity system. He was a textile analyst who had learned from that difficult industry how to successfully invest in cyclical and capital-intensive companies. The economic cycle has been with us for centuries and will continue to be a part of our investment lives for centuries to come. Thus any analyst or investor, particularly one who pursues "growth" investing, needs to understand the ebb and flow of cyclical stocks because all growth stocks eventually become cyclical stocks. Peter's early experience brought him to the attention of Mr. Johnson, who made him an assistant, proving that investment acumen isn't necessarily genetic. Ned may have inherited it, but Peter learned it at the feet of a master. Much has been of Peter's knack for spotting investment opportunities in the real world rather than simply poring over balance sheets and income statements. In his well-written account of his investing exploits, *One Up on Wall Street,* Peter tells us that his wife's delight at discovering panty hose led to his successful investment in Hanes Corp., the stocking manufacturer. In another instance he observed each day on his drive to the office how many cars were parked in the lots at a manufacturer, an indicator of whether production was being ramped up or down. These are great stories with a good lesson, but Peter is far from the only person who used such real-world information. For years I observed the parking lot at a defense contractor, and entertainment analysts I know keep an eagle eye on the parking lots of motion-picture producers.

Certainly Peter Lynch was an excellent investor. But the times were right for him to thrive, the result of the pummeling the market and the economy took in the 1970s. During that period the mutual-fund industry was an endangered species. In 1972 equity mutual funds had total net assets of $55.9 billion. Eleven years later that had shrunk to just $30.9 billion. Much of that decline was due to market performance, but a good chunk was the result of people withdrawing from mutual funds. Between 1971 and 1982 the number of individual accounts in equity mutual funds shrank from 10.9 million to 7.2 million. The industry's dire straits prompted the Securities and Exchange Commission to allow fund companies to use some of their funds' assets to market the funds (12b-1 fees) instead of restricting market expenses to commissions (or loads, as the industry calls them) and management's own resources. Congress also adopted a plan to let individuals save for their retirements through individual retirement accounts (IRAs), a device that the investment industry was delighted to exploit. An added bonus came in the early 1980s when the Labor Department permitted the creation of 401(k) and other tax-advantaged accounts.

Another factor that set the stage for rebounding markets in the 1980s was the final step in 1975 of abolishing fixed brokerage commissions. Prior to that, brokerage firms competed mostly on service and speed of execution, and their focus was institutional clients. Individual investors didn't realize it, but they were getting a nearly free ride on the backs of the substantial fees brokerage firms charged to institutions. Once the fixed fee was gone, competition for institutional accounts devolved into a fierce price war for institutional business. As a result brokerage firms stuck their individual clients with higher fees, contrary to the expressed wishes of Congress. Those higher fees made mutual funds look more attractive to individual investors. The competition for that business prompted many of the larger fund companies to become bigger buyers of Wall Street research products and services as a way to lure customers.

Finally, technology played a role. While stocks and stock funds were in the doldrums during the 1970s, the growing investor interest in money-market funds prompted Fidelity in 1974 to create the Fidelity Daily Income Trust, the first money-market fund that offered check writing. The competition to get customers to buy money-market mutual funds revolved around interest rates as well as convenience, and the money-market mutual-fund business quickly adopted the use of 800 numbers, which AT&T had introduced in the 1960s.

Nobody played all those changes sweeping through the industry better than Fidelity and Peter Lynch. Like most fund organizations, Fidelity in the 1970s generated most of its sales through retail brokers to whom Fidelity paid most of the 8.5 percent commission, or load, that investors paid to get into a fund. But by 1979 Ned Johnson realized that retail brokers and high loads weren't working for Fidelity. He had the foresight to start a discount brokerage firm within Fidelity and essentially bet Fidelity's future on a massive effort to sell its funds through the brokerage firm by slashing the load on Fidelity's funds to 2 percent and undertaking a massive advertising campaign touting both the need for individuals to save for retirement and Fidelity's performance, particularly its high-yielding money-market funds. The bet paid off because Ned recognized before anyone else how the environment in which Fidelity operated was changing and moved quickly—and correctly—to position Fidelity to take advantage of those changes.

All the spending on advertising did its job, establishing Fidelity as the go-to fund family for companies setting up 401(k) and other retirement plans. That started the initial inflows that gave Peter Lynch the ammunition to do what he did best: invest. His subsequent record amplified the advertising campaign and resulted in massive amounts of money being thrown at Magellan. To handle the ever-increasing tide of money, Peter expanded the fund's holdings enormously. In 1980, Magellan held sixty-nine stocks, only a few more than the sixty-five stocks that Ned Johnson had in the fund in 1969. By 1987, Magellan had 1,787 issues in its portfolio. The number of stocks in Magellan was important because it gave the fund a lot of liquidity in case of a sudden wave of redemptions (i.e., plenty of issues could quickly be sold without triggering big tax gains, and Peter could disperse money among enough stocks that his trades didn't instantly become obvious to other players).

But it was the distribution of all those stocks that tells the story of Peter's success. Sure, Magellan held lots of high-quality blue-chip issues such as IBM, and they often remained in the portfolio for years. But Peter also had sizable investments in a lot of much smaller, faster-growing companies such as La Quinta, the low-cost motel chain, and Taco Bell and Dunkin' Donuts, two very dissimilar fast-food chains. Finally, he played to his strength as a cyclical investor with stocks of companies that were not only cyclical, but that were either damaged or highly leveraged. I remember thinking that the strain had finally gotten to Peter in the early 1980s when he placed orders with our firm to buy shares in Chrysler—a company almost everybody assumed was headed for bankruptcy court—at less than $10 a share. And he didn't restrict himself to thinking in terms of individual companies. He would buy entire industries if they were in sufficient distress. At one point Magellan held 130 stocks whose name began with *First* in the midst of the savings and loan debacle. He bet that the government, using taxpayers' dollars, would bail out the industry, and he was very profitably correct.

Besides his ability to ferret out investment opportunities that others didn't see, Peter had two other powerful resources that contributed to his success. First, he had the people skills to get a large number of Fidelity's very competitive analysts to come up with lots of new names of potential stocks to own. Second, he had an uncanny ability to figure out which of the three main areas of the portfolio—blue chips, small growth stocks, and cyclical turnarounds—he should target as new money poured in. His sense of asset allocation—all done in a fishbowl of press and public scrutiny—testifies to his self-confidence (not that Peter was ever arrogant about his success).

There have been four portfolio managers of the Magellan Fund since Peter Lynch left the helm in 1990. Lynch handpicked Morris Smith to succeed him. Smith was an introvert and very religious, which meant he wasn't in the office late on Friday afternoons or on Saturdays. Peter, in contrast, often spent Saturday in the office catching up on his prodigious reading. Smith acquitted himself well in the first year after assuming Peter's crown, beating the S&P 500 by 30 percent. But in the middle of his second year, while running about even with the S&P, Smith responded to a "higher calling" and decamped for Israel to live for the next several years.

The next manager, Jeff Vinik, was brilliant. He soundly beat "the market" in his first year at the helm. Unfortunately, that isn't why Jeff is remembered these days. Recall that Magellan's charter basically allowed it to go just about anywhere and do just about anything in the face of changing conditions. In Jeff's last two years of running the fund, it had grown to over $50 billion in assets, roughly the size of the entire mutual-fund industry back in 1972. But the fund's size wasn't as important as the nature of its shareholders. Over the years Fidelity's heavy marketing of retirement accounts had succeeded beyond Ned Johnson's wildest dreams. Even if an investor didn't own shares in Magellan, he or she almost invariable knew somebody whose 401(k) or IRA was in Magellan. Retirement investors generally are in it for the long run, and they invest in a fund like Magellan to get the higher overall returns offered by stocks. But Jeff took Magellan's mandate seriously—too seriously, perhaps—and when he began to sense that the market might hit some rough patches in the next year, he quietly liquidated a huge portion of Magellan's stock portfolio and reallocated the funds to bonds and cash. In retrospect, it was the right thing to do, and Magellan's charter gave him the authority to do it. But when the year-end statement was issued—before the market had begun to fall as Vinik believed it would—the press and Magellan's investors were shocked to see a fund that looked much different from what they expected. "If I wanted to own bonds, I would have invested in a bond fund" sums up the general attitude. Amid the drumbeat of opprobrium that ensued, Jeff soon left to establish his own phenomenally successful hedge fund.

Next at bat was Robert Stansky, who had been running the Fidelity Growth Company Fund. Bob's selection, I suspect, was at least in part intended to reassure investors that they really did own a stock fund. Bob managed Magellan as a growth fund for much of his eight-year tenure. In three of those years he beat the

S&P 500, and in only one year did its net asset value decline. Bob's performance against other narrowly defined growth funds was even better, and Magellan continued to grow, reaching its peak size of $106 billion in assets in 1999, just before the tech-stock bubble burst. With the big stock market declines in 2000, Magellan also slipped into a decline. The fund has experienced net redemptions every year since, and by the time Harry Lange took control of Magellan at the end of 2005, it had declined to $63 billion in assets. As this is written, Lange's performance has been reasonable—better than the average large-cap growth fund, but not as good as the S&P 500—and Magellan's assets have fallen to $44 billion.

THE LESSONS

Magellan's history embodies lessons both large and small that we should understand. Not all of them apply to everyone, but certainly everyone can find some that will be useful.

1. The environment in which any investment is made is undergoing constant change. That change can work to the benefit or the detriment of the investment. Whoever is managing your money must not only see the change occurring, but make the correct decision about what to do as a result of it.

2. New funds or newly issued stocks have a built-in competitive edge against existing funds or stocks, any of which can, under the right circumstances, experience periods of

remarkable growth no matter how long they have been around.

3. The stocks of highly leveraged companies tend to respond more violently to incremental information. If the information is good for the leverage, an investor can reap large rewards. But if the information indicates that leverage is a detriment, an investor can suffer large losses. More to the point, no one knows in advance whether the next available piece of information will be viewed as good or bad.

4. As Gerry Tsai learned the hard way, no matter how good you think you are at what you do, a family member who is just as good will often have the inside track to the top spot in a family-controlled company. That isn't necessarily bad for the company, just the way it is. Investors should understand that succession will be an issue in any wealth-management relationship and plan for that eventuality. If possible, know who the candidates for succession are and get to know them before the transition to determine if you want to give them a chance or if you need to begin looking toward an orderly transition to another firm.

5. Look around. If you pay attention and think about what you are seeing as you go about your life, you will find investment opportunities. It may not happen often, but when it does, the opportunity can be lucrative.

6. Industry allocation matters. Peter Lynch successfully juggled what were essentially three separate mutual funds within Magellan—blue chips, small growth, and cyclical turnarounds—that each performed very differently,

resulting in a superb blended performance. Jeffrey Vinik reallocated Magellan's holdings to prepare to weather a storm. The nature of the reallocation—he went heavily into bonds—didn't become public until Magellan's regular filing and caught investors by surprise. If you're an investor, you must have a clear understanding of what your allocation is intended to accomplish. If you're managing money for someone else, you must know exactly what they want to accomplish and never, ever surprise them.

7. Have the courage of your convictions. Peter Lynch bet that the government would use taxpayer funds to bail out the ailing savings and loan industry, so he essentially bought stocks in the entire industry, not just one or two players. He also bet that the government would rescue Chrysler Corp. Both bets paid off handsomely.

8. We cannot always know what motivates someone. Peter Lynch doubtless recommended Morris Smith to succeed him because of Smith's innate investment skills and probably didn't know Smith would leave so soon.

9. Most investors want to measure the performance of their wealth managers against that of various market benchmarks. But market benchmarks don't own the same stocks, don't engage in trading, and aren't worried about redemptions. You'll learn more about your manager by comparing his or her performance against that of managers or funds that are pursuing the same strategies and goals. Magellan might not have beaten the S&P 500 every year, but it was often doing better than its actively managed peers pursuing the same strategy.

10. The past is not necessarily prologue. Choosing an invest-
    ment style or mutual fund based on its past performance
    is no guarantee that either the performance or the style
    will continue to succeed or even continue at all. Investors
    need to pay attention constantly to what is happening to
    their investments and to those who are managing them.
11. The best portfolio managers are going to have a volatile
    record. Their highs will be higher than those of other
    managers, and some of their lows will be lower. What
    matters is that there are more highs than lows.

17

TIME AND MONEY:
The Measurement of Value

We make a limited number of purchases that have as their principal worth their current use. They can be as mundane as paying for electricity or clothing or, more significant, such as when we spend money on education for education's sake or the acquisition of a home that we essentially rent from ourselves as the ultimate owners. Most of the rest of our assets we acquire in the belief that in the future these assets will have more value to us than what they cost us to acquire them. The terminal value of an asset is particularly important as the measure of our success as investors. We do not know either the terminal date of our existence or the date on which any other force may end the valuation period. Nor do we know in advance the absolute price we will receive, even before that price is adjusted for inflation and taxes. For example, we know the exact date on which a bond we own matures. But when we buy that ten-year bond, we cannot know how the tax laws will change over the next decade or what inflation will do to erode the value of the bond's principal. We are always dealing with uncertainty as we look to the future. That tends to make us, as rational beings, uncomfortable. Even after we get past that uncomfortable feeling, we must still find ways to deal with the myriad uncertainties that are our future. A few people may deal with uncertainties by ignoring them, but most of us know implicitly that ignoring uncertainties doesn't make them go away and doesn't mute the impact they will have on our futures.

One of the coping mechanisms to deal with uncertainty we have learned from childhood is to relate one thing or action to others. We accept that we do not fully understand what we are dealing with, but we then liken it to some other thing or action that we do understand at least a little better. By our relating one thing to another, our value system begins to grow. As investors trying to assess the future worth of an action or asset, we have been trained to relate it to some other asset or result. Thus, we look for at least two if not more measuring sticks to determine present as well as future value. The academics call this the arbitrage theory of pricing. Initially X is worth Y percent of Z. If the market determines that under some stimulus X and Z should be worth the same, we buy the less expensive one and sell the more expensive one, if we believe the proper stimulus is going to be supplied. (This is particularly true if we can cause the stimulus to occur.)

The trick is the selection of the appropriate other measuring stick to compare the two. In picking our comparison, we need to make sure that the timing of the point when the two measures are estimated to be identical is acceptable, e.g., now, tomorrow, year end, by tuition time, by retirement, within my lifetime, within my heirs' lifetimes, or sometime. There are two general approaches to ascertaining value. The first is the attitude of the trader, which is that something is worth only what you can get for it in the immediate present or close future, i.e., now or later today. This is the approach traditionally followed by lawyers and judges who believe that a fiduciary trustee is carrying out his responsibilities if the assets under his control are disposed of at prices that are equal to or greater than the prices at the time of the trust's inception. A second approach is that of the investment theoretician who believes that an investment is worth today the entire stream of future income (interest and dividends) discounted back from the future for the certainty of the income plus the terminal value of the investment. The discount rate chosen can be as low as the interest rate of a supersafe U.S. Treasury bond of appropriate maturity or as high as the yield on risky junk bonds or even higher. Discounting future payments requires that the higher the rate of discount, the lower the present value of the asset is.

In between the two general approaches—the trader's price today and the investor's expected long-term future value—are two other approaches used by professional investors that look not at the value of the stock or bond, but at the underlying value of the asset they represent, usually a company.

In what I call the mortician's view, one would focus on the value of the body and its various parts, including gold teeth. The mortician looks at a company in terms of its liquidating value. In the most extreme case the mortician weighs the net cash on the balance sheet less all the liabilities and expenses necessary to free that cash. When the net cash is greater than the current selling price of the stock, the mortician sees a "net-net" situation.

As mentioned previously, net-nets were first identified by Graham and Dodd in *Security Analysis,* written about their investment experience and lessons in the 1930s. Because of general disenchantment and distaste for common stocks at that time, a number of these bargains were available. Today fewer net-net situations exist because the searching power of the computer reveals almost all of these potential liquidations to vulture investors. Nevertheless, these opportunities do exist today as balance sheets can at first glance understate net cash assets by overstating liabilities. More frequently, pure cash and short-term, high-quality securities do not exceed the stated liabilities. Today liquidators are well practiced in wringing cash out of troubled companies by obtaining higher-than-book-value prices for assets and reducing the size of liabilities through hard negotiations. Active and skilled company investors are the protagonists in this play, often backed up by a "Greek chorus" of funds and other advisors who either purchase the target's securities and/or provide funding to the activists. While there are more troubled companies in a recession, there are plenty even in rising markets, so this kind of investing is largely independent of general market conditions. The funds and advisors who trade in this type of merchandise view themselves as "value" managers, for they have specific values for each of their investments independent of the general market. Historically, Michael Price's Mutual Series Funds and The Third Avenue Funds have used these techniques effectively. When they are successful, the returns on individual positions can be outsize, but timing of the returns is often in the hands of the courts or otherwise difficult to predict. In a well-diversified portfolio of funds or separate account managers, this kind of investing has a place, particularly given the relatively low risk of large capital losses.

The second approach is that of an art buyer who believes that "beauty is in the eyes of the beholder." The value-in-the-eyes-of-the-beholder approach rests not so much on the value of the present assets, but on the expected value of the assets and income in the future. The practitioners of this approach are not slavishly extrapolating past trends forward into the future. They are betting on favorable changes either in the fundamentals of the company's business and/or in the pricing mechanism for the company's securities. Most often the focus is on changes to the results produced by the company, not the price/earnings ratio or some similar metric. The changes that analysts and professional investors look for start with top-line revenue numbers that can rise faster than the historical experience due to favorable changes in selling prices or greater unit growth that may result from existing or new products or services. Investors next look for increased value in cutting costs. These savings can come from a more productive labor force, often with focus on a more productive sales force relative to their compensation. Other areas of potential savings are lower-cost production techniques and/or lower raw materials costs. In some highly financially leveraged cases, lower interest rates can have a dramatic impact.

The formulas for improving results are reasonably well-known, but may not be followed by present management for numerous reasons. These include lack of new products or services, insufficient capital, inability to attract the required talents, unfamiliarity with critical technologies or new ways of doing business. In all likelihood the stock market's present valuation on the company recognizes these limitations. At this point the art buyer's thinking comes into play. The question becomes what would a knowledgeable corporate operator pay for the company in its present condition. In numerous circumstances a buyer would be willing to pay a premium price because of perceived advantages often based on a very uncertain belief in synergism. The estimated premium price is often calculated by examining other transactions in the public or private markets. These prices represent value to some professional investors. They will buy stocks at prices below these value metrics and either passively or in some cases actively push for transactions by a knowledgeable buyer who will recognize the value. Mario Gabelli is a master of this methodology and uses it to guide many of his Gabelli Funds. Since these kinds of deals are not always available, this approach requires considerable patience. Mario is a disciple of Ben Graham's, as are Warren Buffett and Irving Kahn. Each of their portfolios follow these approaches, but one finds little if any overlap in the specific names they own. Yet each is viewed as a value manager.

Still other approaches to value are practiced by some world-renowned investors. John Neff, when he was managing the Windsor and Gemini Funds, used the growth of earnings power to define value. He reconstructed both the income statement and the balance sheet of a company to eliminate nonrecurring accounting and operational items, then projected this defined earnings power into the future. He also added the dividend yield into his calculation of terminal value. Sir John Templeton, a global investor of more than seventy years' experience, believed that over long periods valuations around the world would converge. He successfully invested for U.S. fund shareholders in foreign companies whose price/earnings ratios were well below those of comparable U.S. companies with somewhat less good prospects.

The term *value* thus encompasses a constellation of concepts that relates the worth of various investments to something other than the current price of the stock in the search for bargains. Each of these approaches has worked to the long-term advantage of investors and should play a role in the portfolio structure of wealthy, risk-conscious investors.

18

THE RACING FORM:
The Art of Performance Analysis

T he fallacy of using market and economic aggregates loved by columnists, teachers, salespeople, and lawyers is based on sound-bite summarization that oversimplifies what is happening and why your experience can and should be different from the aggregate result. The art of performance analysis is based on understanding the misleading dangers of focusing on aggregates.

Much of my career has been spent measuring, mostly the performance of mutual funds. I started as a securities analyst in the 1960s and determined early in the game that among the 150 or so mutual funds that existed then, the ones that were performing the best would grow the most and be the most likely to expand the names in their portfolios and, therefore, be the most willing to pay for my research. To determine my sales targets, I started to calculate fund performance. Most of my number crunching in those early days was on the back of envelopes. In 1967, after working as an analyst at a bank and two brokerage firms, I joined the brokerage firm my brother founded as an analyst and director of research. I quickly got an additional responsibility to sell the first computerized mutual-fund performance analysis to mutual funds and other institutional investors. On December 5, 1968, the SEC took the first step to end the fixed-brokerage-commission era. Brokerage commissions had been the principal way our clients paid for our services. By Thanksgiving 1971, my brother decided to leave the brokerage business. In mid-1973, he sold the mutual-fund data bank to me for a big balloon payment. Lipper Analytical Services was born, with its first weekly performance analysis at the end of June 1973. My timing was exquisite: mutual funds were managing roughly $54 billion when I bought the business and were within 18 months managing just $34 billion. Luckily for me and the investing public, today at least nineteen long-term funds are bigger than the entire mutual-fund business of those days.

Not to downplay the significance of what Lipper Analytical Services became over the years, but the easiest way to understand what I did is to know that in my youth I spent some successful hours at the Thoroughbred racetracks. For the mutual-fund industry I essentially re-created the racing form, an analysis of past performance and other valuable information with the hopes of upgrading statistical and narrative information to useful intelligence. Earlier mutual-fund performance data existed to aid fund salespeople. What my brother's firm did was to create the first computerized data bank to aid multiple sorting of the same data. Over the years Lipper Analytical expanded its activities and products, adapting all the time to changes sweeping through the financial services businesses, including longer trading hours (which gave us less time to calculate and get results to *The Wall Street Journal* on an exponentially growing number and type of funds), international investing, and shifting regulations. We were constantly developing new products and services for the industry and running up against rising expenses. A new product that might have cost $100,000 to develop to the cash break-even point in the 1970s was, by the 1980s, much more expensive. By the 1990s, development costs for new services were in excess of $1 million. In the mid-1990s, my guess was that a decade hence the annual development costs would reach $10 million. A new product had no guarantee of financial success. For me, the risk as a sole proprietor was becoming too large. In addition, I had long told myself that I would sell the business when I began to reach my level of incompetence. Further, my span of control was stretched too thin with five offices, including London and Hong Kong, each doing different things, and employing more than three hundred people. In the summer of 1998, after two years of discussions on supplying data or joint-venturing distribution outside the United States, I sold the operating assets of Lipper Analytical to Reuters Group Ltd.

What I learned about the art of performance presentation and analysis over those twenty-five years has helped me and my investment advisory accounts for more than forty years understand performance motivation and made me a more successful investor. To some, a discussion of the art of performance and motivation seems a little quixotic in a field mostly described in precise numbers. The difference between these two viewpoints is an understanding of the differences between precision and accuracy. Precision is an exact mathematical measure often calculated to many decimal places, e.g., a fund is up 12.345678 percent over the last 250 trading days. Investors will believe that over the lapsed time the gain was on average exactly 12.345678 percent, and because of the precision they are likely to have enough faith that they will extrapolate forward the 12 percent gain, particularly when compared with another fund that had an 11 or 13 percent gain. They might feel a great deal differently if they learned on average each day the fund moved up or down 25 percent. An entirely different view would be generated if most of the trading year the fund was up 100 percent, then went into precipitous decline through a series of daily losses. Recognize in all three examples the terminal performance could be equal at 12.345678 percent, but a sawtooth pattern for the 25 percent daily moves, or a chart of a high plateau ending with a sharp decline, could well be considered a more accurate analysis. Through all those years I have observed how many smart people have used measurements. Among the most important things I learned was not just how to measure and what to measure, but also how to use measurement. Height, for example, is an important measure when you are recruiting for a basketball team. But if you are looking for a world-class chess player, height is probably meaningless. Measurement can also help refine definitions. Consider that since basketball point guards tend to be closer to what we consider a "normal" height than centers, it is easy to see that the universe of potential point guards will be somewhat larger than the universe of potential basketball centers.

The fundamental lesson is that measurement is a tool not so much used to provide answers, but to help you ask important questions. Hopefully the questions asked lead to a greater understanding of the thing being measured. That understanding may or may not lead to better decisions, but I am thoroughly convinced that bad data more often than not leads to bad decisions. Bad data is often a symptom of the absence of quality control and a management lacking prudence.

For the wealthy individual, certain measurements are more important than others. How well the Dow Jones Industrial Average has performed so far this year is, for example, of far less consequence than the difference so far this year between expenses and income. More complicated is the measurement of one's need for contingency reserves compared to one's marketable securities. The complication arises because most wealthy people should be planning for multiple contingencies ranging from the immediate to the long-term. Going a step further, measuring the ratio of one's marketable to nonmarketable investments should yield useful information. There are no "right" answers, only information that one can use to make judgments about the adequacy of various assets and the wisdom of their deployment.

Many measurements are "hard" measurements, stated in dollars, percentages, or some other numerical metric. But "soft" measurements, which cannot easily be quantified numerically, are also important. Psychic gratification is one of the most important soft measurements. I will use the example of my cowriter, who understands full well that his ownership of a forty-six-foot sailboat has no "hard" investment value—after maintenance and insurance it is indeed the proverbial "hole in the water"—but which provides clear psychic gratification that is worth the financial expense. When using performance measures or hearing someone else use them, one should be as aware of the psychological facets of measurement. The premise of the successful Broadway musical and subsequent motion picture *My Fair Lady* is that a person's language may classify that person. That is certainly true in the world of investment, where the choice of words and viewpoints classifies people. When one hears someone talking about the percentage decline from a peak price or the percentage gain over a particular period, an agent is probably speaking. Agents are most often motivated by their need to avoid career risk. The risk they fear most is being terminated.

In the early years when an agent is new to the business, he or she invests considerable money, time, and effort in acquiring clients. In later years as the agent trains his clients to use his time more sparingly, the agent's productivity goes up and the account increases in value to the agent. If the agent is contemplating the sale of his office, many potential acquirers will be willing to pay more for the long-term accounts in the belief they are less likely to be driven away by the change of ownership.

Under normal circumstances when the stock market is rising, the agent and his long-term clients tend to have brief conversations or presentations that revolve around the notion that "we" are doing well. The account is up some percent from a prior peak or from the last quarter. Even when performance rolls over and starts down, the focus remains on how "we" are doing: "We are only down a small amount." Unless there is some reason for concern, both the agent and the client are happy to move the conversation on to other topics. This "measuring from the top" tends to cast market performance in an optimistic light, implying that there will be higher highs in the future. Measuring from the bottom, contrasted to measuring from the top, will by definition always produce a positive number. It is the agent's fallback position in times of extended trouble. Bottom-up measuring gives the investor the perception that he or she is progressing toward one or more goals, no matter how distant. While agents tend to prefer measuring from the top except in times of duress, investors themselves tend to measure from the bottom because that provides them with a feeling of success. The fact remains, however, that whether measured from the top or the bottom, the current dollar value of the investor's account is the same.

A third way of looking at performance is from the inception of the relationship or the initial transaction. For many years courts have determined whether a trustee has acquitted his responsibilities adequately and should or not be surcharged or forced to rebate the trustee's fees by measuring performance from the inception of the trust. Another way to think about this method of measurement is to look at performance using total-return accounting, which takes into account the reinvestment of income as well as market gains or losses. Total reinvestment of all income and distributions is the preferred way to compare different managers. However, if total reinvestment is not how the account actually worked, other measurement approaches are likely to be more appropriate. Measurement from inception is commonly used to determine gains and losses for tax purposes. Since in most cases involving investments that have been operating for a few years or more the initial investment will be the lowest valuation or close to it, "measurement since inception" is similar to measurement from the bottom.

If our clients are willing to focus on and discuss an array of statistical performance data concerning their investments, we typically start with current-period performance, which, while topical, is often not insightful unless it shows an unusual pattern compared with other periods of up-and-down markets. We also show other longer-term periods that are more useful for comparison. Finally, we almost always show performance since inception.

All this discussion of performance measurement misses the point most of the time. The purpose of performance analysis is not to provide answers about whether a fund or a manager should be retained. The purpose of this and kindred statistics is to aid in posing questions about what is going on in both the marketplace and the portfolio manager's head. These factors will influence future performance, not historical baggage. Only then can the investor, with the help of the portfolio manager and other advisors, develop an informed guess about whether this particular investment will fulfill the long-term need for this portion of the investor's account.

19

THE ESSENCE OF TRUST:
Selecting Wealth Managers

S electing the people who will help you manage your wealth is one of the most important decisions you can make. Too much is at risk—your wealth and, perhaps more importantly, your financial psychology—to approach the selection cavalierly. One of the blessings of wealth is that it allows you to seek better solutions to your problems, often by using specialists. That's certainly true in your financial life. Too much information is available, change is happening too quickly, and the world is too competitive to rely on a single advisor to handle all your investment needs as well as your taxes and your trusts and estates. These are the people who will guide you or actually make investment decisions for you, your loved ones, and your charitable works. While the selection process can be short or lengthy, it is always intense because you are making commitments and asking others to make them as well.

Selection begins with determining what you want from a manager. Most people judge potential managers based almost exclusively on past performance. They look for managers who have outperformed some benchmark. That's a big mistake, both because the analysis of performance is more difficult than you think and because a single-minded focus on performance necessarily neglects other important facets of the client-manager relationship.

I have known some of the best investment managers over the last half century and a few of the worst. They all experienced their own best of times and their own worst of times. In fact, some of the poor managers have turned in better performance during their best times than the good managers produce in their best times. The critical differences lie in the frequency of good times and bad times, the depth of the bad times, and the ability to differentiate fads from fundamental changes in the marketplace and in the nature of the companies whose stocks and bonds the managers buy and sell. We can only learn about those differences over reasonable periods of time. Three years or less is not reasonable. Four years, the span of a presidential cycle, is the minimum (the largest equity mutual-fund management group today uses a four-year period for incentive awards). Corporate executives and former Communist Party members both advocate five-year plans. Maybe they're onto something. But even that may not be long enough to show the effects of both up and down markets on a manager's performance. In any event performance is only one tool in selection, and it is used mostly as the grounds for discussions with potential advisors about reasonable expectations.

While you should not ignore performance, a more important

criterion for selecting a wealth manager is how much influence you want to have over how your manager manages your money. By "influence" I mean your ability to persuade a manager to take into account your preferences, such as broadening the universe of available assets, to manage your account to minimize tax liabilities, or to pursue a socially responsible investment program. You may be willing to ride through storms or you may prefer that your manager take you out of the market as storm clouds gather, albeit at the risk that you may not get back in at a better price.

Getting and using influence is a balancing act for both you and your manager. From your point of view you have to be a significant but not overwhelming part of your manager's business. If your portfolio constitutes less than 1 percent of the total amount he has under management, you will have no real influence. Up to about 5 percent you slowly gain the ability to have your manager act on your wishes. At 10 percent I guarantee he's paying attention to you. But at some point after that you may become too big and exert too much influence, posing the risk that if you withdraw your business, the management firm might have to lay off people or even close down. Perhaps more important, the manager may not have the courage to stand up to you and fundamentally disagree with you and thus will become less valuable to you as an "independent" advisor.

Some managers will welcome your input and others will not. One way to get an idea about a manager's willingness to accommodate you is to ask about the "dispersion of returns" among his or her accounts. That's a fancy term for how widely the results in the various accounts he manages vary from one another. A money manager who is trying to attract corporate business and is thus dealing with consultants has a vested interest in keeping the dispersion of results narrow, to demonstrate that new money will be treated just like old money. You will not have much influence with him.

Communication is critical and has to be clear and unambiguous. The goal of communication between you and your advisor is the management not so much of money as of expectations. If you expect higher returns than a potential advisor believes you can get, you need to know that. Similarly, your advisor needs to know what lies behind your expectations, even when they are realistic.

If you're comfortable with the jargon of investment, finance, taxation, and trusts, that's great. You and your advisor can throw around obscure terms all day. But if you are not familiar with the lingo, be sure a potential advisor speaks plain English and is able to explain concepts in terms you completely understand.

Communication must also flow both ways. A good money manager should interview you at the same time you're interviewing him. A fixed-income manager, for example, should want to know if you view the value of the fixed-income investment as the income it generates, or do you look at it on a total-return basis, including appreciation? Is volatility of income important to you? How would you feel if the manager takes a loss?

The manager's interest in you should be at least partly selfish. A good manager will not come out and say it, but it should be clear from your interview that he's trying to figure out how much extra work will be involved in satisfying your investment objectives. Do you, the potential client, have your life under control, or will you be constantly changing your investment philosophy to fit the latest crisis in your life? Are you, the client, willing to admit making mistakes and willing to recognize that your money manager will make mistakes? A manager who does not appear to be interested in those things is probably more salesperson than money manager, interested more in getting you to sign on the dotted line than in ensuring that you will be a good long-term client.

Good management comes at a cost. Traditionally, the money-management industry has been compensated by charging a fee that is a percentage of the assets—usually around 1 percent or less on larger accounts. But the rise of hedge funds and private equity funds in the past few years has created a new compensation model based on performance. Managers of such funds can be paid 20 percent or even up to 50 percent of the profits they return in addition to a management fee of 1 to 5 percent. For those managers who perform, the rewards are enormous. Indeed, the profit-sharing model is so lucrative that many of the best portfolio managers, analysts, and traders have left asset-based funds to play in the new realm.

The nature of the compensation structure radically changes the nature of the relationship. While traditional managers are essentially your employees, managers who earn performance fees are your partners. In fact, they are your senior partners, and you will have little or no influence on their activities. The only thing you can do is add or subtract money from your investment fund at prescribed times. If you wish to influence your managers, performance managers are not the total solution you need. They can, however, play a role in part of your investment program.

Just as investors like diversity in their portfolios, many want diversity among their managers. Among professional investors I see a lot of "horse races" in which they hire two or more different managers and pit them against one another. A better approach for individuals is to hire complementary managers who take different approaches to investing and can be expected to have different results.

If you decide to have three or more managers, you might consider hiring a "supermanager," someone to oversee and coordinate your other managers. Since a supermanager will be responsible for the overall returns of the entire portfolio, it may be hard to find someone for that position. Most managers would be unwilling to take responsibility for returns not under their control. But should your supermanager be responsible for a portion of your portfolio or should he be an independent expert riding herd on the account managers? Sports offer a useful analogy in the forms of coaches and player-coaches. Player-coaches have the advantage of current experience in the trenches, and many a sports team has effectively been led from the field. A coach, on the other hand, may never have been a star, but often has the wisdom and patience to see and develop talent as well as encourage teamwork.

The best way to deal with the player-coach/supermanager is to indicate that his share of your assets will be limited to the current share except as influenced by performance, and that he will be judged on how well the entire portfolio does in meeting the various goals set out for it. Many and probably most managers want to be judged only on those investments that they directly command and will thus not accept the supermanager role. In that case or perhaps initially you may be better off with someone who has invested widely or has had managers or funds of different natures and proclivities report to him.

All of this requires considerable effort on your part, not only to determine potential candidates, but also to understand your own objectives, preferences, and style. A good manager for one person is not necessarily the best manager for someone else. Choosing the wrong managers can be a financial disaster or merely a low-grade annoyance. Choosing the right managers can lead to a long and profitable relationship. As with so many things in life, you get the managers you deserve.

20

HERE LIES DANGER:
The False Allure of Trading

Most investors, at one time or another in their lifetime, try their hand at trading stocks or other financial instruments. If you pay attention to nothing else that I have written, pay attention to this: don't trade with a lot of money. The odds are heavy that an attempt to trade profitably will over time lead at best to a useful experience of manipulation of emotions.

We know gambling has a tremendous allure. Why else would Las Vegas casinos exist? And millions of people willingly gamble despite knowing that the odds are in the house's favor. Trading is not gambling but akin to it. My guess is that the percentage of traders who enjoy success is higher than the percentage of gamblers who are successful, but not by much, because of the substantial costs associated with frequent trading. Trading is fast and exciting, quite unlike the slower, occasionally glacial, pace of investing. But without carefully developed and honed skills, trading is a fool's game.

I need to examine the myriad pitfalls of trading to demonstrate why I urge most people to shun trading. Start by recalling our initial comparison of investing with physics. Friction—the equivalent of costs in the investment world—requires that any input produces a smaller output, the difference being lost due to friction. Trading involves the payments of commissions, fees, taxes on gains (the deduction of net losses from your taxable income, remember, is limited), and information sources, at the least a real-time source of prices.

Trading involves lots of errors, committed by the trader and his agents. No one talks much about errors, but they happen every day on even the most professional trading desks. A trader executing an order for a client buys or sells the wrong security, buys too much or too little, buys at the wrong price or at the wrong time, or simply does not follow instructions. All of those things are manageable, but they do generate additional costly friction.

All that, however, is just a prelude to the real cost of trading: the trader's time and emotions. The inattentive trader is tomorrow's cabdriver. A person who trades is akin to a jockey astride a racehorse, who must be extremely conscious both of time and the horse's relative position. A moment's lapse of concentration and the other horse is passing on the inside of the second turn. Imagine riding a horse in the Belmont Stakes. The luckiest jockey—that is the safest—would be left at the gate while the pros swarmed down the first straightaway before making his move by passing tired horses in the stretch of the longest race for most horses in the United States. To be a great jockey takes tons of practice and the experience learned from lots of lost races. The same is true of traders. Truly skilled traders are few. Those who survive should never stray from their knowledge base. One might be able to trade oil futures well, but that does not mean one can trade bonds with the same hope of scoring big. If stocks are more familiar, one might learn to trade big caps well, but that will not mean one should venture into micro-caps.

Think, too, about the environment before beginning trading. In today's extremely dynamic and competitive environment it becomes hard for the skilled professional trader even to explain in detail the theoretical underpinnings of what makes him successful. Often a top trader knows little about the investment fundamentals of the security he is trading, and that is okay. He is looking for differentials in momentum, watching the combination of moving prices and volume to decide his next move. To do that successfully requires quantification skills and a good bit of knowledge of specific market history, as well as an indefinable "feel" for how things are happening at the moment. The best traders are amply rewarded for their skills and occupy the proprietary trading desks at the biggest securities firms and hedge funds. Increasingly, however, even the seasoned pros are being shoved aside by computers, which can process millions of times more information than the human mind and make ever faster decisions about whether to buy or sell. These proprietary-account traders and the computer-driven trading systems trade against all other market participants.

To be sure, in small stocks that trade in modest volumes—stocks that "trade by appointment" is how the Street describes them—one won't literally be overwhelmed by the big trading desks and their computers. But those stocks are so small and the volume so thin that one can't make much money by trading them. Once trading in sufficient volume to make money commences, the pros are likely already trading the stock.

To be successful, an individual trader should have the same skills and access to the same information as the pros. If you do not have those skills and access, do not trade. The game is rough and getting rougher every day.

Now take a more restrained view of why one should not trade. Trading is not an alternative to what we commonly call investing. Investing is the selection of an array of assets, each with its own place and purpose in a long-term portfolio. Trading is the intense focus on a single asset type or class with only one purpose: to make money quickly. A good investment is one that, if the price falls by half, one should want to buy more. If the price doubles, one may want to consider reducing the size of the holding. A trader, on the other hand, upon seeing a price moving in the wrong direction for even a short time, may be wise to liquidate that holding. An investor should always have some investments in the portfolio, even when conditions are not right and cash seems like the best haven. A trader sometimes needs to have no exposure to any positions.

As I hope this comparison suggests, investing and trading are two different things. Too many people confuse the two. While a good trader can make money faster than a good investor, a bad trader can lose money faster than a bad investor, and the odds are that a bad trader will lose a *lot* of money faster.

As I said at the outset, do not trade at all, or if "the thrill of victory and the agony of defeat" is so powerful, do it with a small, a very small, portion of your wealth for a short period or until the losses are big enough to be painful.

21

A CONTRACT, NOT AN ASSET CLASS:
The World of Hedge Funds
and Alternative Investments

Caveat! I know a little about this topic. First, I am one of two managing members of a narrowly based domestic financial-services hedge fund that is not appropriate for most investors. In addition, I am a direct investor in five hedge funds managed by others. In accounts we manage, we use some hedge funds sparingly. Further, a number of the nonprofit organizations on whose boards I sit use or have contemplated the use of an array of alternative funds. There. Now you are aware of what may perhaps be a biased view, albeit one based on some knowledge.

In modern financial parlance hedge funds are most often referred to as an "asset class." That definition is plain wrong. Hedge funds are not in any sense of the words an asset class. True, they deal in a variety of assets, but those assets are the securities or vehicles in which they invest. Bluntly put, hedge funds are nothing but a contractual fee arrangement between the funds' managers and their clients. The arrangement grants to the managers potentially large incentive fees while the investor's money is locked up for a contracted time.

Hedge funds have long been considered glamorous, a reputation gained in no small part because Alfred Jones, widely considered the "father" of hedge funds despite that none of his techniques were new. He was a writer for *Fortune* magazine in the 1960s. Not surprisingly, *Fortune,* as well as other business publications, played a large role in subsequent years in creating the aura that surrounded investors in hedge funds. That aura was enhanced, as many things are, by the exclusivity of the limited access. Regulators placed restrictions on who could participate as an investor in hedge funds based on the size of the investor's wealth as a way to protect the investing public who might not have adequate professional advice. The size of one's wealth was the sole determinant if one was a "sophisticated investor." And only sophisticated investors could be accepted by these funds if they were to avoid registration with the SEC, which does not permit the profit-participation incentives that make alternative funds of all types attractive. Unfortunately, the regulators confused wealth with sophistication rather than requiring accumulated knowledge or wisdom.

Historically, the wealthy were attracted to hedge funds as a means to participate with specific managers, to use difficult investment vehicles, or to take advantage of certain esoteric investment styles that were not available to less "sophisticated" investors. In addition to wealthy individuals or families, nonprofit groups such as foundations, universities, and pension plans sought hedge fund managers' talents.

Soaring demand for hedge funds in the past several years—an estimated nine thousand hedge funds exist in the United States today, and more abroad—has been as much a fashion trend as a financial trend. Nevertheless, that demand has fundamentally altered the nature of these investment vehicles. When discussing hedge funds, it is easy to make generalizations that, like many generalizations, are far from accurate. The very word *hedge,* for example, is a gross generalization. Alfred Jones's initial hedge fund was set up to be 50 percent long the market and 50 percent short and thus "hedged" against general market moves in either direction. That sounds like a reasonable strategy until you realize that the market is dynamic and that the fifty-fifty balance so carefully set up immediately begins to erode as prices move up or down. To be truly hedged would require constant—and expensive—rebalancing. More important, however, most hedge funds today are no longer really hedged within the market for their own instruments. They are instead vehicles for different kinds of often esoteric investment instruments that the sales force presents as a "hedge" against other kinds of common investment instruments, such as a stock portfolio.

The appeal of hedge funds has in recent years been driven by the perception among wealthy investors that it has become more difficult to find good stock investments, particularly in large-cap domestic stocks. These investors seek out hedge funds in the expectation of higher returns. The early hedge funds were mostly oriented toward stocks; hedge funds now invest in other types of securities, commodities, and nonpublic companies, as well as objets d'art and derivatives of all types. Lately many funds have become oriented toward fixed income, in part because they can "safely" use much more leverage than is allowed in the stock market. Further, fixed-income markets are larger, there appears to be more certainty about the behavior of fixed income, and a given manager can manage more money with fewer people.

Hedge funds rely on secrecy, the lack of transparency of their transactions, leverage, and portfolio holdings. Investors perceive that in exchange for granting potentially large incentive fees of 20 to 50 percent of profits plus a base annual management fee of between 1 and 5 percent, they are getting specialized knowledge from the managers and access to some financial instruments and strategies that are not available to others. To some extent that perception is correct because no two hedge funds are exactly alike, and given the secrecy in which they operate, it is exceedingly difficult to compare two hedge funds without investing in both.

Many hedge funds thrive on the use of leverage. Leverage is created by using someone else's money, at a cost, to add to one's own resources to buy assets. Leverage is a familiar concept if you own a house with a mortgage. But hedge-fund borrowing is somewhat different in that it is much more fluid and often more extensive. The levels of borrowing, asset coverage, and interest rates can and do change daily, for better or worse. If, for example, the assets in a margin account decline to near the value of the loan, the lending prime broker or bank will demand more collateral or a reduction in borrowing within a day or possibly less. The lender has the right to liquidate a portion of the collateral to bring the loan level back to a proper balance. Most often the big lenders are financial institutions with capital-ratio requirements that drive their lending practices. Typically, such margin calls are made in a time of stress, particularly when the general market is declining, causing individuals and leveraged funds to sell long positions, or to cover short positions. These actions tend to exaggerate the general volatility in the market. The best way to think of leverage is that for an investor it can be his best friend and his worst enemy. While some hedge funds have little leverage, some funds that invest mainly in currencies can have as much as ninety-plus times leverage, i.e., the amount borrowed is equal to ninety-plus times the amount owned by the investor.

Many hedge-fund managers come not from the world of investing as much as from the world of trading, particularly the trading desks of the biggest and smartest securities firms. Most managers of public securities come from the more numerous ranks of securities analysts. Given the relative scarcity of smart and successful "graduates" from the big proprietary trading desks, it should come as no surprise that investors believe they are paying for unique talent and unique strategies. But what those investors do not fully realize is that only some traders leave the trading desks to set up hedge funds, and they may not be the most experienced. The traders that remain know what the hedge-fund managers know and do not hesitate to take advantage of that knowledge. One of the lessons in the collapse of Long-Term Capital Management in 1998 was that in many instances the proprietary trading desks of the large brokers owned as much of similar instruments as Long-Term Capital. When the crunch came, the trading desks—which the hedge funds relied upon to execute their trades as well as, in some cases, to provide credit— were at a tremendous advantage over the troubled hedge fund.

I believe hedge funds will continue to thrive despite the recent subprime debacle, which has attracted much attention to the funds despite that relatively few were directly involved. Partly that is because the hedge funds' salespeople explain away things like the Long-Term Capital Management collapse or the more recent subprime crisis as "a hundred-year storm." Since we have just experienced one, it will be a century before another occurs, they argue. Gullible investors ignore that these hundred-year storms seem to be occurring a lot more frequently than once a century. It is more like once every six to ten years. Investors also are misled by terminology. The subprime crisis, for example, was a surprise because some of the infected credit paper held by the funds was rated AAA. The subprime layer was held in an instrument along with a majority of its assets of AAA quality. Investors saw the AAA ratings and ignored the subprime component, unaware—or unwilling to be aware—of the toxic nature of the subprime portion in 2006–7 mortgages. The problem with the subprime portion lay in the collapse of underwriting standards as Wall Street firms and other financial companies muscled their way into the mortgage market taking market share from the traditional banks and thrifts. Market share was won by letting credit standards decline. The result was no-down-payment and "no doc" loans, a development that many of the traditional lenders then mimicked. As long as the vast majority of the subprime borrowers paid their mortgage notes there was no significant problem. But when the homeowners began in large numbers to delay payments or failed to make them, the system unwound, hurting some of the so-called sophisticated investors, among others.

Hedge funds can and do in many cases make sense for some

portion of wealthy, sophisticated investors, including nonprofit institutions. The three keys to using them wisely are to invest with moderation, understand what you are investing in, and find portfolio managers with sufficient talent to overcome both the price and the reduced liquidity of hedge funds.

How much to bet on a hedge fund is similar to the question of how much to bet on a horse at the track. Small bets that result in small losses are disappointing, but not catastrophic. With a large amount kept in a hedge fund you run the risk of encountering one of the increasingly frequent hundred-year storms and thus jeopardizing your ability to accomplish your life goals. Keep in mind that big losses tend to occur after big gains. Much of the danger in hedge funds lies not in the original investment, but staying with it after achieving way-above-average gains. Since hedge funds usually require a lockup period of up to two years, you may have to spend a year or so with bated breath hoping that your redemption hour arrives before the next big storm. (Other alternative funds often have lockup periods of ten or more years.)

I cannot emphasize enough the need to understand the risks and instruments that a hedge fund you are considering can be expected to use. Much of this information will be available in a fund's offering documents, albeit clothed in opaque legalese. An experienced professional advisor can be used here to great advantage. A good deal of information is also available in the periodic letters that the general partner or manager sends to investors and that legitimate prospects can obtain. But merely obtaining the letter is not enough. You need to read it, think about it, and be sure you understand it. And once you have made the investment, you cannot afford to fall asleep. You need to track whatever relevant hard data is available, and you need to be sensitive to what is being written or talked about. You are not trying to second-guess the manager, but you are trying to determine if the size of your investment remains appropriate to your purposes. I am an investor in a hedge fund with a short bias, and my research indicates that when the manager is wrong, the fund is likely to experience a 20 percent loss in that year and, in some cases, a 50 percent loss would not be shocking. Obviously, I think the fund will be up in more years than it is down, but I know I can accept the down periods when they occur. I expect my investments in a distressed-securities fund to be less volatile and have a performance lagging the economy.

If a fund has sufficient history—that is, it has gone through at least a few market cycles—you will obviously have a better picture of the manager's abilities in up as well as down cycles and the nature of the instruments the fund uses. But with the enormous growth in the number of funds that kind of history is becoming increasingly rare. Keep in mind that market cycles for investors in the stock and bond markets are less disturbing because it is easy for an investor to get out of either market. That is not true of hedge funds in general. Be aware, too, that over time the nature of a hedge fund may change, at least in part because the manager often keeps his incentive compensation invested in the fund. A successful manager will, as a result, have a substantial sum and the preponderance of his or her net worth riding on the performance and may, consciously or not, become more conservative over time. If you are a latecomer to the fund, you might want to assume that its earlier strong performance may now be trending more conservative. Such a trend is not a standard evolution, but you should be aware of it.

You should go into a hedge fund, as with any investment, with some rationale for getting out. My approach would be to note when I invested what percentage of my market-related net worth the hedge fund represents. If that percentage in the future doubles or triples, I would begin to think it appropriate to dial back my exposure to the original level. This is not suggesting that the fund will not continue to do well, but rather that I have introduced an unbalanced element into my portfolio and need to rebalance. I would tend to feel that more certainly if I am a fiduciary investing on behalf of a trust for heirs or charities and less certainly if it is my own money at stake.

Finally, I would have firmly in mind an expectation of the fund's performance. If that performance exceeds my expectation in either direction, I would seek to understand why that is happening. If I cannot solve the intellectual issue, I would be tempted to withdraw at the earliest opportunity. In 1998 after I sold the operating assets of my data-publishing company, I was looking for investments and numerous people urged me to look at Enron. I studied the company's 1997 annual report and could not figure out how they could be making that much money out of the assets I saw on the balance sheet. As a result, I passed on the opportunity to buy Enron. If you do not understand the game, do not play. That little piece of advice may have saved me more money over the years than my actual knowledge of investments has made for me.

Hedge funds have drawn a lot of notoriety lately, some of it justified. But the real ranting and raving should be directed first at investors who did not know what they were doing and second at the salespeople who do not present a balanced view of the product they are offering. Frequently a more balanced view can be found in the offering documents, but too many salespeople dismiss the importance of and take advantage of the difficulty in reading those documents, much to the eventual regret of their customers.

This discussion of hedge funds is an appropriate place to also touch on other "alternative investments." The lockup period for many hedge funds is up to two years. When we examine other alternative investments, we find lockup periods are often ten or more years. You have less liquidity in an extended lockup, and you are also much more exposed to the lack of published prices. The manager is investing in things that do not trade often. Indeed, the last trade may have occurred so long ago that it no longer has any relevance. For these alternatives to be competitive with hedge funds, the rates of return should be materially greater. Yet, some of these alternatives will have components that prove worthless, an unlikely occurrence among most hedge funds. Good hedge funds are analogous to baseball players skilled in singles and doubles and scoring when the market environment is favorable to them. Other alternative investments are more like home-run hitters, who score with one swing of the bat. Just remember that many home-run hitters also have a high percentage of strikeouts. The year that Babe Ruth hit the long-lasting record for home runs is the same year he set the record for strikeouts.

If anything, the relative skills of the managers of alternative investments should be higher than those of the hedge-fund managers. Now we are beginning to talk about some exceptional people. The question is, are there enough of them around to adequately manage the demand for such investments? For example, someone interested in investing in art will find that the skills of the expert who concentrates on eighteenth- and nineteenth-century oil paintings are very different from the skills of someone managing investments in twenty-first-century 3-D objects. The Old Masters expert knows the history of the paintings, knows the potential buyers, and can consult experts in forgery and insurability. The expert in new art objects has less of that. Buying a work by some undiscovered artist who is later discovered can provide returns that are multiples of the percentage gains in Old Masters, but you can probably put more money to work in Old Masters.

Private equity is another area getting a great deal of attention recently. While there is no legal definition of what constitutes private-equity investing, it is understood to largely be investing in companies that produce enough cash flow to sustain more debt than they are carrying and that need time to further develop their business before they are sold or resold to the public. As we are all aware, most public-company management is focused on quarterly or annual earnings and on attempting to maintain an orderly growth in those results. A private company need not be concerned with quarterly or annual earnings, only with growing the basics of the company in terms of client capture, revenues, new product development, and personnel development. All of those things are more likely to pulsate rather than flow. The management of a private company can willingly destroy an earnings progression to acquire whatever is needed this year to improve results two or three years from now. Such a company could be attractive to a private-equity group who could provide enough time, capital, and, in some cases, expertise to build both the business and the financial record with the idea of selling it to a strategic buyer or taking it public.

Private-equity investors may be either individuals or funds. Individual private-equity investors know and are known in a particular business, such as the oil discovery and drilling businesses. Funds, on the other hand, can be linked to an industry or can simply go dialing for dollars, looking for private companies that want an infusion of cash and, in some cases, management expertise. You will know well enough if you are qualified to be an individual private-equity investor as a result of your network and expertise. If so, you will almost certainly have a sufficient understanding of what you are getting into. If you find you must become part of a fund to invest in private equity, keep in mind that the lockup period generally lasts until the last investment is sold or taken public. That can seem a long time.

Some private-equity funds own a wide array of investments. These are often groups that were started within the investment-banking sector, by brokerage firms or sometimes banks. These funds are often organized on a vintage-year basis, so that if you put your money in today, you will be in the class two years hence. That means that you will not participate in the maturing investments prior to that. It also means, to some extent, that you are investing in a blind pool because you do not know what investments the group will be making with your money. Such an investment requires a great deal of faith in and understanding of who is managing the fund.

Finally, venture capital has a certain appeal among the wealthy.

Venture capital comes in three basic flavors, the simplest of which is angel investing. You meet an inventor, you like his story, and you give him some money to allow him to build the business plan or perhaps a simple prototype. Next is the seed-capital phase, in which money is used to get a company organized as a going concern. Finally there is mezzanine financing, which is the money needed for the company to reach maturity and get positioned for a sale to a strategic buyer or an initial public offering. The risks and returns of venture-capital investing are calibrated to whatever stage you choose as an investor. The majority of angel investors will presumably lose money frequently, but all they need is one hit out of twenty to do well. Seed-capital investors have more evidence of the viability of a business but may have lower returns earned in less time. They start with proof of product and finish with proof of business. Mezzanine money then takes over and carries the company to the point at which the venture is ready to stand on its own feet. The mezzanine period, spent preparing for the sale, is relatively short. Funds exist at both the seed-capital and mezzanine levels, and some funds may exist at the start-up level, although they tend to consist of proven people known to one another.

Overall, I believe an investor who wants to participate in these exotic alternative investments needs to take a far different approach to such an investment than he or she would toward investments in such liquid instruments as common stocks and bonds. You may want to enter one or more of these realms if you are building a financial structure that has a ten- or twenty-year time horizon or that is multigenerational. Still, whatever money you invest should be written down to zero in your mind because you have no practical way to recapture that money to pay bills in the foreseeable future. I can also see using this kind of investment in some nonprofits that can afford a long-term view and don't need a cash return quickly.

As for antiques, art, and other nonfinancial instruments, I would advise you to invest only if you get psychic enjoyment out of finding extreme bargains or can savor the pleasures of owning an object with no regard to financial consequences (which, of course, is not investing, but enjoying). And when your friend Joe comes to you for money to fund the development of his exquisitely complex widget, invest at your own risk. You will likely lose both your money and your friend. And remember, finance and fashion are two different things. Never invest in anything because it is fashionable.

PART THREE

LOOKING
AHEAD

22

A PARALLEL REALITY:
Developing My Forecasts

Specific or implied forecasts are built into all investment decisions. We know that forecasts have little chance of being completely accurate, but they are usually one of the foundations for our investment actions. The first two causes of risk—overconfidence and unanticipated events—should be filters through which all forecasts are viewed.

People who provide forecasts are first and foremost people. To avoid the embarrassment of appearing wrong to others, forecasters seek comfort from history. I have said that if you scratch most analysts or economists, a historian will bleed. History is known, but less than we believe, and the future is uncertain. When we are being indoctrinated with history, we are not told about present or future studies of researchers using archaeology, astronomy, biology, and contemporaneous literature searches, all of which can often contradict or seriously modify what we believe to be historical facts. Nevertheless, most forecasts are built on the backs of the historical record.

While we know that the world is made up of quantitative and qualitative readings, forecasts are almost always expressed in numerical forms, often ignoring critical relationships that are primarily based on qualitative factors. In the simplest form most forecasts are stated as one or more numbers. We tend to believe that the greater the number of numbers, the better. We tend to confuse precision and lots of numbers with accuracy; that is, being correct. The more sophisticated forecasters offer up multiple scenarios that grow at high, medium, or low rates. Almost never do we see graphs that show parallel lines, and rarely do we see an "elbow" on one trend but not on the others. This confusion between precision and accuracy leads to overconfidence. To produce such precision, one has to know a great deal about the future.

The "history trap" becomes even stronger if the forecast is from someone who was right the last time, or worse still, the last couple of times. This confidence is reinforced if the forecast is a simple extrapolation of the recent past in the almost Newtonian terms that an object in motion will stay in motion. From my viewpoint the recently successful forecaster is more likely to be wrong. The more difficult task is picking out the forecaster who has evolved a different set of assumptions or, better yet, a more enlightened set of data. At least in this way I am on guard against overconfidence.

The second cause of risk to forecasts is the likely occurrence of unanticipated events. Applying this awareness to forecasts, like good technical analysts, we should search out signs of major reversals. If we have been enjoying good weather for years, be prepared for the hundred-year storm. U.S. stock markets, on average, move in four-year cycles, often related to the presidential election cycle. Thus, after three good or bad years, one should start to look for a reversal. You may not be able to find the proximate cause, but that will not prevent the reversal from occurring.

From an investor's viewpoint multiple forecasts of varying lengths of time are needed. Some such periods are the remaining taxable year, the period until tax payments are due, the remaining part of the calendar or planning year, the current presidential cycle, a five-year planning period, the period before the next significant planned withdrawal such as college or school tuitions, down payments on houses, or funding a new charitable initiative, the period to retirement from present job, time to ultimate cessation of economic production, your and your spouse's or partners' actuarial event, longevity of heirs natural or institutional or life spans of children, grandchildren, or great-grandchildren.

The sources for these forecasts are likely to be as varied as the periods. Publicly available sources for the current periods are found in searches of pronouncements by brokers, banks, politicians, columnists, and surveys. Your accountant can help you determine the exact date when taxes are due. Actuaries and doctors may be of some help for many of the periods. You may well have to come up with your own forecasts. After you have reviewed the accuracy of other forecasts, you can take some comfort that you will probably not come up with materially less accurate forecasts than those of the "experts." The key is not the initial forecast, but the reviewing for midcourse corrections. You may be wise to use a single day of the year—your birthday, for example—to set your review.

It may be helpful for me to explain how I develop my own forecasts. I begin fully cognizant that forecasts are subject to a lot of biases: what is included and specifically excluded, how reliable the data is in past precision or future accuracy, how various factors are weighed, what the frequency of updates and revisions is, the determination of a benchmark to judge whether the forecast was a success.

I am primarily interested in making investment decisions on the selection and retention of funds, separate account managers, and individual securities. I focus on absolute price changes adjusted for distributions of dividends, interest, and realized capital gains after all account expenses, but before taxes. Relative performance is of secondary interest to me, but useful in understanding the risks and rewards of tactical choices. For me, the best universe of data is the mutual-fund data provided by my old firm, now known as Lipper Inc., a subsidiary of Thomson Reuters, augmented by my more than forty years of making good and bad investment decisions for myself and others.

Why do I focus on a less important universe than the national or global economy? A study of the progress of GNP (gross national product) and various stock market indicators show that for sustained periods of time they move in different directions from one another and almost always at different rates of change. Lots of variables can lead to divergences between the performance of the economy and the net earnings of companies. Some of these variables include labor and capital productivity, which is another way of expressing operating and financial leverage, nonuniform price changes throughout the economic chain, innovation and tax realization, plus leads and lags within the economy as well as inventory adjustments. Each of these variables moderates the linkage between the economy and a company's net income. Some investors use net income as a starting point for their investment decisions, but a study of reported earnings or future estimated-earnings trends are not coincident with security price trends. The missing link between earnings and stock prices is the supply of and demand for investment dollars. These are in turn driven by the demand for investments to fund future spending versus the supply of securities to fund present spending. This tug-of-war can be identified in different valuation metrics, such as price/earnings ratios, price/book value, price/sales, and price/EBITDA, all of which are used to justify the current price either relative to historical prices or a competitive use for the money. At the beginning of 2007 "bulls" on the stock market acknowledged that a slowing economy would lead to slower growth in earnings, but they believed this negative would be more than offset by higher valuations caused by buyers seeking investment opportunities, thus pushing up price/earnings ratios and therefore stock prices. That scenario was the reality with which they were dealing at the time.

I prefer to deal with what some may call a parallel reality. I start with the current prices reflected in the assembled portfolios of funds. What others think about valuations and the future are already captured. I need to decide how accurate I believe these current prices are as a picture of the future in whatever the time horizon of my investment objectives.

In building the statistical matrix for a forecast, I tend to look at both period-by-period (usually year-by-year) figures as well as longer-term aggregates of five, ten, fifteen, twenty, twenty-five, thirty, and thirty-five years. Why do you have to do both? Because you will draw different conclusions from each set of data. For example, do S&P 500 index funds beat the average U.S. diversified mutual funds? At the end of 2006 an examination of the data show that index funds won over the last two years and the last fifteen years. However if you look at the data on a year-by-year basis, you would see that the index-fund average had not topped the managed-fund average between 1999 and 2006. Further, the superiority of the index fund in 2006 was about 3 percent. This relatively large gain will stay in the calculations for the next several years, which will distort the conclusions. So much for the data side of this particular question, and this would be the result if you sorted the answer with just a computer.

I believe data is only an input to finding the answer. What you need to learn is why in 2006 did the S&P 500 index outperform? The answer, I believe, comes from an understanding of how the institutional-portfolio-management business works. Most investment books are, in theory, written from the individual or institutional-customer viewpoint. You will not find in most of these books one of the big risks that operate throughout the marketplace globally: career risk. Career risk is the risk that a portfolio manager will lose his job due to underperformance of his fund or accounts relative to a securities benchmark, as unfair as that comparison may be.

In early 2006 a number of observers believed that earnings were peaking and would be followed by lower stock prices by early May. Many more feared a broad economic slowdown. Those fears began to be realized in late 2007 and early 2008. The great advantage of the individual investor over the institutional or professional investor is that the individual can get out of the game at any time. Not only can the institutional investor not leave the game, he will be judged against other institutional investors as well as market indexes. Under those conditions, experienced institutional investors prize the liquidity normally available in large-capitalization stocks. That liquidity gives them the flexibility to sell quickly without a substantial price penalty in case of a large redemption or withdrawal from the account or when a great bargain appears, as is often the case in down markets. So many dollars sought refuge in mega-cap stocks that the S&P 500 index was driven close to its peak levels.

The lesson here is not that large companies are inherently better or cheaper than midsize or smaller caps, but that their stocks provide more liquidity. When the fear of a major decline finally abates, the odds favor that market leadership will shift back to stocks with less liquidity.

Forecasts should not be stated as single-number targets, but should cover ranges of returns. I develop my ranges by averaging the compound growth rate of U.S. diversified funds—representing more than seventy-five hundred funds with assets of $3.8 trillion—over two, three, five, ten, and fifteen years. The compound growth rate of this aggregate was 9.67 percent, close to the average for the S&P 500 index funds, which had lower costs because of lower turnover rates. To build a range of forecasts I take half of the average for the low point, or 4.88 percent, and add the same amount over the midpoint for the high of the range. Based on current data, the range would therefore be 4.88–14.5 percent. While this range is higher and lower than any of the annual averages, my experience reminds me that some individual years were more extreme. I handle these historical outliers by using the approximately 5–14 percent range for two-thirds of the time. Half the individual years will fall within this 5–14 percent range. Approximately one-third of the time, a single-digit decline will occur. Roughly one-fifth of the time there will be an abnormal year, which occurs once in a ten-year period, when the gains or losses reach 25 percent. Once every approximately twenty-five years (often after a decade without a 25 percent move) the "Big One" hits, a move of 50 percent up or down. Bear in mind, these average ranges are for diversified domestic equity mutual funds. More specialized portfolios or funds managed with unusual skill can perform differently. Forecasts of investment performance should, to be useful, cover a greater variety of investments than the forecasted range developed above.

One way to beat "the market" is to have a concentrated portfolio of equities. Such a portfolio might hold a limited number of securities, say twenty to forty issues, or it might be invested in one economic or industrial sector. A number of portfolio managers run both a concentrated portfolio as well as portfolios that have a larger number of issues. Watching the spread in the performance of these twins, we see that few managers add significant value by sharply limiting the number of securities they hold. One exception is Ken Heebner at CGM (Capital Growth Management). The more typical concentrated portfolio is focused largely on a single sector. Currently the major sector classifications include a catchall "specialty/miscellaneous" one. On average the sector bettors appear to have an advantage of between 2 and 4 percent compared with U.S. diversified funds over time. Over multiple years the extremes can be wide, ranging from 1 percent to almost 32 percent. On a single-year basis, the extremes can be truly breathtaking, from down 95 percent to up over 100 percent.

As consumers and investors, we do not live only in the United States. We have been exposed to domestic companies that derive a substantial portion of their revenues from overseas trade or from operations based overseas. Many Americans are increasingly investing globally (anywhere in the world, including the United States) or internationally (outside the United States). The attractions of investing beyond our borders are, briefly, the chance to own different kinds of businesses or those in different stages of their investment life, cheaper valuations, and the impact of foreign-exchange price movements. These benefits have become increasingly attractive over the last five years with gains over the U.S. diversified equity funds of 2.3 percent to 3 percent. I view this increment largely as a currency-level benefit that over longer periods largely disappears. There may well be, for a while, an advantage in investing in the smaller less developed markets. Of the $5.3 trillion in open-end SEC-registered equity funds, some $1.3 trillion is invested in funds that invest primarily globally or internationally. Thus, on average, American investors, individually or collectively, have about one-quarter of their money exposed to foreign markets. Nowadays no investment forecast should be without a foreign-exposure component.

At the other extreme is forecasting fixed-income-fund performance. The difference between the performance of equities and bonds is often called a risk premium. The larger the gap, the greater the perceived risk is believed to be for the equity owner. Using the same multiyear-average approach, the equity premium averages about 4.7 percent, with higher numbers in the last several years.

What does this all mean? I believe we can conclude that well-chosen investments in individual securities, separate accounts, or funds offer enough scope to fulfill minimum retirement and charitable-giving accounts. How one should convert forecasts to expectations and then actions will be discussed in the next chapter.

23

OVER THE HORIZON:
Emerging Trends
in Wealth Management

he only thing I know with certainty about the future is that it is coming and begins right now and goes on forever. When one of the distinctly different futures arrives in full force, most of us will not recognize the change, and few of us will have the same description of it until close to its end. Thus I am hesitant to project too far into the future because I have no special expertise in that arena. Unfortunately, few others do either. Nevertheless, there are ways to wisely think about the future that can affect how we act today.

I am by nature optimistic. Therefore, I am willing to get out of bed in the morning. On the whole I think the events that have occurred in my business and investment lifetimes, whether financial, political, economic, or social, have been overwhelmingly positive for me and for much of mankind in general.

Nevertheless, it is appropriate as a risk-conscious investor to look first at the dark side as the pace of global social and economic changes continues to accelerate. The changes that occur will displace people from their familiar settings in society and the economy. We have seen that happen here in the United States over the past several decades as auto, steel, and other industrial workers have lost their relatively high-paying jobs to technology and competition from overseas, as well as from right-to-work states. Many of these displaced workers have found other jobs, albeit at lower wages and with less lucrative benefits. But some have not found work. One problem is lack of mobility—they cannot or will not leave their homes for venues that have job opportunities. The mind-set of others among the unemployed or underemployed dictates they cannot accept a position at less pay than they earned before ("I was worth it then, I am worth it now"). Their failure to find work has not much affected our entire economy. The jobs lost at General Motors and Ford have been replaced by jobs created by the Googles of the world. But they are different jobs that require different skills, and they have been taken by different people. For the autoworker looking for a job in Detroit, what happens in Silicon Valley may as well be happening on the moon.

The sad fact is, some people in the United States and around the globe may have to be considered "residue" from the bubbling economy. Some do not have opportunities to become a productive member of society, and others, for whatever reasons, reject the opportunity. The residue also includes the seniors without productive work, a population that will continue to grow as a percentage of U.S. and European populations. What are we to do as a society when we have 10 million or more people over the age of one hundred? These people will still have the right to vote. They will also be big consumers of health care while being essentially unproductive economically for thirty years or more. As a nation we are rich enough now that we can pay for the current generation of the residue, but in a highly competitive global economy, we will not be able to afford it to the fifth generation. This sad scenario does not even begin to consider what is happening now and what will happen in the future in the dysfunctional parts of the world that have little in the way of government services and no real economic infrastructure. As progress accelerates everywhere else, these places, mostly in Africa, will fall farther and farther behind with higher humanitarian implications that we must view with trepidation. I do not know the solution to this problem and there is no guarantee that one can be found. But I do take some encouragement from the knowledge that a few people are searching for solutions. Faculty members at MIT's Media Lab a few years ago launched an initiative to develop a $100 laptop computer, a technology that could revolutionize education for the world's children living in poverty. That is a start, but much, much more will be needed, and I foresee a growing role in this arena for nonprofit organizations funded by donations of dollars and talents.

With the exception of some sections of Africa and some other parts of the developing world, I believe that we are leaving behind the era of personal geography. While most of us still think of ourselves in respect to our own geography, including national boundaries, we are becoming much more citizens of the world, buying and selling our goods, services, food and minerals, and intellectual property beyond our familiar time zones and borders. Multinational corporations have known for years that where you are headquartered is not nearly as important as your ability to communicate globally with customers, suppliers, investors, and employees. Communications will increasingly depend on computers, satellites, and network connections of all types. Because we will live in an increasingly interconnected world awash in information, there will be far fewer secrets between people, companies, societies, and governments. That will probably be a net positive, but I can also foresee the problems that arise in a global economy from increased usurpation of intellectual property. If a creator expects his creation's profit is going to be denied him, there will be far less incentive to create or make intellectual property available to others.

That geography will become less important is highlighted in the nature of the biggest problems facing us as we hurtle into the future: climate, health, energy, and food. We are once again beginning to understand the implications of a global economy founded on and operating on limited acceptable fuel supplies. The scientific community has the ability to understand the nature and extent of those kinds of problems and to begin to formulate solutions. I am a little more worried about the ability of the economic community to adapt either to the problems themselves or to the solutions. Can Ford and General Motors survive in a global auto industry that prizes efficiency—both in production and operating costs—rather than marketing expertise? But I am most worried about the ability of political institutions to understand and respond to these problems.

Yet another problem confronting us is the determination of the values that will guide us—and by *us* I mean the world—in the right direction. Religion through the centuries has been a powerful force for both good and evil. Right now we are witnessing a fundamental clash of religions globally. While the problem seems to be creating instability, the real problem is the huge difference in values underlying the conflicting religions. As disruptive as these conflicts are and will be, the people of the world are likely to accommodate to a working solution, one likely to involve a transfer of technology and other values.

On the positive side, the opportunities are great, but less well defined than the challenges. Focusing only on areas of some personal professional knowledge, I believe we must develop new ways of thinking about investing as well as new ways to identify and manage risk. We should be able to find ways to reduce risk without a proportionate reduction of rewards.

Information should also influence the kinds of companies that dominate the investment universe. Marketing of personal success has been the single strongest differentiator among investment firms over the past few decades, but that may change as research-intensive enterprises find ways to participate earlier in successful investment opportunities.

The nature of investments will change, too. Investing is about capital creation, the process by which good ideas are developed and brought to market. As we have witnessed over the past decade, there is no shortage of ideas emanating from the growing global entrepreneurial class. Today, some fear that we will run out of good new innovations, a new idea to them. One hundred or so years ago there was talk about closing the U.S. patent office because everything of significance had already been invented. Going forward, there will inevitably be more Googles. Just as surely, many, indeed most, new ideas will fail as businesses in their early development. One must pick one's investments carefully.

I believe that equity—the ownership of a stake in an enterprise—will be with us far into the future. One cannot imagine a better way to bring together capital to achieve a goal. But much of the equity will be in the form of amalgams, either managed actively by fund managers or deployed through passive vehicles. We will see a vast proliferation of trading instruments under the rubric of equity, from common stocks to esoteric derivatives and even outright royalty payments. While others may want to take the risks of profits, one might prefer to collect a portion of revenues instead as a safer bet than earnings.

The rising number of entrepreneurs in practically every corner of the world will force opportunities into view. There will be no shortage of ideas, but there will almost certainly be a shortage of qualified management talent, an opportunity itself. Managing well requires experience, and there will simply be too many new enterprises for the existing number of qualified managers to run. Failures will not necessarily be the result of a bad idea, but of a good idea mishandled by inexperienced or incompetent managers.

Inflation will continue to be a part of the economic picture, waxing and waning as it has for centuries. The problem with inflation is recognizing all of its sources and manifestations, as well as understanding the implications inherent in whatever is causing inflation. In the 1960s the United States suffered from wage inflation due to the shortage of qualified labor, some of whom were unavailable because they were deployed in Vietnam, while others were kept out of the job market by lack of education. Today we are suffering a shortage-induced inflation created by bottlenecks in the discovery and production of resources such as oil, copper, natural gas, and other minerals. Future inflation may be caused by government borrowing too much so as to fund expanded health care for our growing population of retirees. But what I think we will become more concerned about over time is the hidden inflation that cannot easily be seen or is not measured and thus takes its toll unnoticed. For example, when you go to your doctor or dentist, much of your time in the examining room or in the chair is taken up explaining your malady to a nurse or doctor's assistant, yet you wind up paying the bill for that time at the doctor's or dentist's rate. It is akin to Hershey's old practice of keeping the price the same while shrinking the size of the candy bar.

I suppose my most esoteric notion about the future is that we will need to find a way to carve out time for contemplation. Right now we seem energized by exploding technology. Who can imagine not having a cell phone and BlackBerry at hand virtually twenty-four hours a day? I certainly thrive on that kind of access to information, but I also find that I value the respite that occurs on Thanksgiving or Christmas Day, when there is little new market information to parse, people are not in their offices or working at their desks at home, and things get relatively quiet (how quiet being a function of how large your family is). Perhaps in the future, when geographic boundaries have eroded considerably more than they have today, there will be designated havens—perhaps a cluster of islands in the Pacific Ocean or a scenic resort in the Himalayas—that by international agreement will be free of cell phones, sat phones, pagers, and even television and radio. While this Shangri-la will be wonderful, please briefly tell me about it when you return for I will be focused on the untold opportunities that the future will bring to create, manage, and protect wealth from a rising tide of better educated and smarter people (which are not necessarily identical) who believe that their desired shares of rewards will come from our share. The biggest opportunity that I see is to make the overall pie bigger. The way I can do that is by prudently finding increased operating leverage in the financial community, and by reducing the frequency of avoidable large losses through the better use information turned into useful intelligence. As in my earlier work, I will be developing or using more efficient racing forms for the world's activity.

✦ LIPPER'S LEXICON ✦

T his lexicon or glossary is unlike most the reader will have seen. I have assumed that you have a good dictionary to get the literal definitions. Below is a list of terms that have been sprinkled throughout the book. By each term is my instinctive reaction to the term and perhaps a speck of insight on how a wealthy individual should think about the term. My hope is that it can spark some thinking and provide good ammunition for your next investment discussion.

Accountant—The person who, if competent and kept adequately informed by the client, should know where the money is, how it got there, and what it will cost to move it somewhere else.

Advisor—A professional whose principal contribution to a financial relationship is the ability to make decisions with less emotion and more knowledge than the client.

Angel investor—One who provides seed money, often to a family member or friend, to fuel the development of an idea that may become a product, service, or company. Angel investments are highly risky, and an unsuccessful investment is likely to cost the investor not only money, but also a friendship.

Annual meeting—An elaborate ritual in which shareholders and management meet once a year for an uncomfortably long time during which each tries, mostly unsuccessfully, to pretend that the shareholders actually own the company and have some voice in its management. In the past these events were essentially picnics with speakers and opportunities to see the company's latest products, but that level of civility ended some time ago.

Asset—The ownership of property, real or intangible. While often thought to refer to concrete or financial holdings, talent, when it is in demand, is an extremely valuable asset. In the financial community the most prized asset is the float on somebody else's money, i.e., the money held for someone else that can be invested for your own return. The float does not appear on your balance sheet, but the proceeds of its use accrue to your income statement.

Asset allocation—A highly touted process in which one's financial holdings are spread over several different asset classifications on the presumption that price trends in the different classes will differ in both direction and magnitude, thus providing some degree of protection against a calamity in any given class. The original data that supported the use of asset allocation was both naïve and flawed. Subsequent data is hardly convincing.

Balance sheet—In its simplest form, a listing of assets and liabilities, an exercise in which we all engage when we list the pluses and minuses of a given situation, such as making any significant purchase. In financial terms, a balance sheet represents the accountant's view, based only on historical costs, of what a business is worth as of a given day. Balance sheets are by their nature incomplete and can be misleading if one does not read the accountant's certification and, more important, the footnotes. Indeed, skilled analysts frequently read the footnotes first. Just as the wealthy are more concerned about the current sources and uses of their money, for many purposes the statement of net-cash-flow generation that used to be called the statement of sources and uses can be a better operating guide than a balance sheet.

Bond—Derived from the document of biblical times that permitted the ownership of people. More recently, it has come to mean a contractual lending relationship that, much like a mortgage, presumes the timely payment of principal and interest. The global market for bonds, being much larger than that for stocks, is the playground of many traders who attempt, sometimes successfully, to extract higher returns from bonds than anyone has the right to expect.

Broker—A financial actor whom many perceive to be responsible for persuading clients to buy or sell financial assets frequently, but who may, in reality, best serve clients by persuading them to remain invested in bad times in sound investments so that they will be positioned to profit from the inevitable good times that will follow.

Capital—Assets over which you have control, though not

necessarily ownership. A manager of a $3 billion fund may have none of his own money in the fund, but is nevertheless viewed by the marketplace as possessing $3 billion in capital and is treated accordingly. Capital includes intangibles such as intellect, talent, and social and business networks.

Charity—The giving of time, effort, or money to aid those currently less fortunate or to promote certain values. Charity begins at home, but can extend beyond national boundaries. Formal charities are often designated as not-for-profit and contributions thus are tax-deductible. Charities operate with varying degrees of efficiency and rely on the wealthy not only for donations of money and time, but also for advice and contacts.

Deflation—See INFLATION.

Depression—Differs from a recession in that a recession is when your neighbor is unemployed and a depression is when you are unemployed. While a depression is often considered a recession carried to extremes, *depression* is in reality a psychological, not an economic, term. It is the condition in which people have given up and no longer seek to improve themselves through employment.

Discretionary account—A relationship based on faith in someone else's talent and judgment predicated on the notion that one does not attempt to do brain surgery on one's own brain.

Diversification—The principle that underlies asset allocation. The fundamental appeal of diversification is to provide a cushion against sudden price drops of particular assets, but the costs involved in diversifying may well outweigh any gains. Cash and short-term U.S. Treasuries are the only assets likely to be an effective cushion for nearly every difficult period. If one knew what was the best single investment, that would be the only security owned. Since we mere mortals do not know the name of the single best security, we seek to buy more than one security, hoping to capture the first, second, and third best performing. Assuming that one finds the best two and invests equal amounts in each, the resulting performance will be less than the performance of the single best-performing security. Thus the use of diversification is at best a bet and should, like all bets, be used judiciously.

Efficient market—An idealized view of public financial markets, developed by my old client Burton Malkiel, that holds that the current price of a security has within the price all available information and therefore at the moment represents the fairest price. While this is a good starting point for explaining markets to students, the efficient-market hypothesis fails to take into account such phenomena as "the weight of money," in which an investor who is right about the future and is seeking to buy one hundred shares of a security is overwhelmed by a seller who is wrong about the future but seeks to sell ten thousand shares of the same security. Two investors, one seeking to sell and the other seeking to buy, may also simultaneously be wrong or right about their view of a price if they have different time horizons, for example, one day, and ten years. The efficient-market advocate believes the next price will be similar to the last price, the only difference being any new information that has arisen; the speculator compares the current price to what he believes the price will be a short while from now; the investor compares the current price to what he believes the value will be at some future date far away; and Warren Buffett evaluates the current price compared to the value of holding the security forever. Sometimes each of these techniques works.

Fear—The feeling that one or some of our needs are not going to be met in our lifetime. In terms of the financial markets the base-level fear is running out of money, time, and talent to meet our needs. In our increasingly competitive world, other fears are the loss of respect due to poor performance. We fear that our essential companions will lose respect for us if in matters critical to them we do not perform to an acceptable standard. Love may be replaced by scorn and, eventually, hate. This fear of loss drives most people in the financial community to be highly competitive in most things they do, be it getting the right seat on a commuter train, at a concert, or sporting event, or getting the right golf score or investment performance.

Fiduciary duty—The responsibility a professional or individual assumes to put the interests of clients, family, or charity ahead of one's own profit opportunity, if charged with being a fiduciary. Not all agents and many fewer principals have a fiduciary responsibility to a client or someone on the other side of a trade.

Forecast—A prediction or series of predictions about future events. To protect your reputation, don't forecast. If you must, forecast often and wittily.

Greed—The amassing of a warehouse of resources against the risks undertaken to provide against our fears. Notice that fears drive greed, not needs. Some of the most aggressive "players" are those who have already achieved great wealth, sufficient for their and their living heirs' lifetimes, yet they continue to compete. They could be playing for matchsticks as long as they were competing against other champions. Their claim is that they like to compete and they are good at the game. I suspect the real reason that they play is that they fear being out of the game and losing the respect of their close companions because others may forget who they were and therefore who they are. A good antidote for these tiring warhorses are charities and educational efforts. Both fear and greed can drive people to take on greater risks than required to meet their reasonable needs. Coinvestors should be aware of the impact of excessive fear and greed on the judgment of those who share the same investment with them.

Hedge fund—A compensation scheme that permits the manager to participate in the profits of the account.

Heir—The ultimate beneficiary of unearned income excluding whatever portion of an estate that goes to a spouse or caregiver, who very much earned it.

Income—Narrowly, money coming to you. More broadly, a reduction in your debt, such as when the bank forecloses on your home, taking your asset, but also relieving you of the debt owed on it. Most broadly, the psychic benefit that accrues from your own accomplishments and those of your loved ones.

Inflation—A general trend of rising prices driven either by excessive demand or rising costs that gradually saps the purchasing value of consumers and businesses. Inflation is often difficult to detect and even more difficult to combat. Ironically, efforts to fight inflation often result in its opposite, deflation, which is even worse, since a trend of declining prices can result in widespread job loss and social destabilization.

Initial public offering—The first time the public has a chance to participate in an investment, and the first time that the company offering its stock has to make public a large amount of information about its operations that is correct or at least not fraudulent. Most IPOs arrive unheralded, provide meager, if any, returns, and occasionally slip from view forever. The highly publicized IPOs that soar on the first day may be evidence that the issuer and the managing underwriter intentionally mispriced the offering to attract attention and lay the groundwork for a much larger offering of more shares in six months or a year. While a wonderful source of cocktail-party chatter, IPOs should, at most, be a minuscule part of any investment diet and are often best purchased in a pre-IPO period through an investment in a well-managed mezzanine fund.

Insurance—A financial agreement in which risk is shifted from an individual to a pool. Insurance is expensive if the need for it never arises, but well worth it if the need does arise. The insurance policy is only as good as the credit of the issuing company and its willingness to pay claims, and only an expert can properly interpret the policy and the company's likelihood of paying.

Investor—A person or institution that, with others, really does make the world go around by providing the time, effort, or money to make something happen. Investing is the current commitment of time, effort, or money in expectation of future gain, although that gain is often uncertain and difficult to measure in advance.

Lawyer—An advisor whose principal duty is to stop you from doing things you might want to do. A lawyer's advice is derived from the past and is seldom attuned to the future.

Liability—Not only what you owe others, but what you owe yourself in the form of retirement planning, establishment of contingency funds, education for yourself and loved ones, and charitable donations. These are liabilities in the sense that they constrain your use of assets.

Liquidity—In financial terms, liquidity is the ability to quickly convert an asset to cash to meet immediate needs. One often pays too much for liquidity, in terms of upward performance or large discounts, during periods of distress.

Load—A sales charge that is one of the costs of getting advice and administration for those who wish others to provide these services.

Management—The people who oversee and control the resources, including most importantly the human resources, used in corporations, nonprofits, and government. The overriding issue confronting every management is the time horizon toward which they operate. Too often that horizon is the next event that might cause a change in management, be it a retirement, completion of a large transaction, or the next election. While investors often complain that management is too focused on the short term, those investors have failed to design the appropriate measures and incentive to drive management in another direction. While it is widely believed that shareholders have a vote via proxy in determining who will select the directors and thus the management of a public company, the fact is they have two votes, the proxy being the least effective. The other vote is their ability to sell the security. In other words follow the "Wall Street Rule" of selling something one does not like. If enough shareholders sell their shares, the price may fall sufficiently to force a change in management by a determined outside group. Be careful of valuing an existing management group as distinct from their record. Warren Buffett cautions investors that so-called good management can not succeed well with a bad business.

Money—One of a number of assets a person can hold. While perhaps the easiest of assets to measure, it is often far less valuable than skills, talents, and social and business networks. The principal value of money for most people is that it buys someone else's time and, hopefully, the talents of others. While in theory I could fix the plumbing in our house, my wife has concluded it is much cheaper and far more efficient to spend money to bring in a professional plumber.

Mortgage—Once believed to be an ironbound commitment to repay a loan used to finance the purchase of real estate, this has more recently become an option to be exercised by the buyer depending on whether his speculative gamble is working. More broadly, an act performed now in the hopes of achieving a perceived need at the expense of future choices. People often mortgage their future by an action now that precludes choices later, such as marriage and choice of career.

Mutual fund—A public form of group ownership of stocks characterized by the daily posting of a net asset value, the purported value of all the stocks held in the fund. The NAV is one of the great fictions of all time since it presumes the entire fund could be liquidated at that last stated price, when in reality such a liquidation would almost certainly result in a substantial reduction in the value of the stocks held in the fund due to the fundamental law of supply and demand.

Need—The single set of complex systems that drive our motivation. We all are conscious of our need for food, water, security, sleep, companionship, and some form of legacy.

Net income—The money you have left after deducting your debt payments and liabilities from your gross income over any given time. Many wealthy people actually have negative net income, i.e., more money is going out than is coming in. This is no problem if the person intends to spend down wealth, but often comes as a surprise to those who do not have that goal. Negative net income that is not reversed creates the risk that a person will not be able to meet one or more short- or long-term goals.

Objets d'art—A series of asset classes on which the principal return should be the pleasure of ownership. Whether it is a good investment is a function of time and price. A generally successful investor in art wants to be one of very few buyers and, at the end of the holding period, one of even fewer sellers. Rarely will art throw off sufficient cash to meet operating needs. Naïve art lovers who wish to become collectors need professional help to avoid forgeries and learn the provenance of the art in question. Unfortunately most of the really knowledgeable experts reside in the dealers' and auction houses and have a strong advantage in that they represent other buyers and sellers as well as in dealing for their own and related accounts.

Politics—The art form of accomplishing deeds through other people who think they are accomplishing their own goals when in reality they are actually accomplishing your goals without your fingerprints on the weapons of destruction. The game of politics is such that any number can play from two on up. The game, or more correctly, the games are played in each grouping, mob, crowd, or what can be called an organization, be it a company, charity, religious group, multifamily dwelling, single family, or various forms of government. The two favorite tactics are shifts and trading. Nothing is what it seems to be. Attacks are normally oblique and start with rolling up the flanks by attacking juniors first. The recognition of politics is essential to all forms of life and particularly to those involved with money and love.

Portfolio—A collection of assets, liabilities, and responsibilities. Each person can be said to have a portfolio that includes his own talents, personality, and relationships as well as other resources. More narrowly, our financial portfolios contain our financial assets and liabilities to which our and others' talents are applied. A portfolio is assembled by the wealthy when the need arises to change their focus from a single source of wealth to include other assets and liabilities. Going forward, it is the asset-weighted portfolio performance, not solely the one big position, that will determine whether they will continue to amass or lose wealth. A well-managed portfolio should be diversified so that some prices of assets are rising while others are lagging. In a portfolio in which all components rise simultaneously, all components may also decline in unison. Courts, under the prudent-person rule, suggest that some diversification is an important risk-reduction technique.

The Racing Form—A daily newspaper for the serious handicapper (frequent bettor on Thoroughbred horses). *The Form* has many pages of detailed past-performance information on horses running today on tracks around the United States. Some well-written comments about horses and races provide additional color to the statistics. *The Form* was my intellectual model for the beginning of mutual-fund performance analysis. In both cases, I found that it was important to note the prevailing conditions—weather, distance, and competition, for example—of each race to determine how well or poorly a horse or fund performed.

Real estate—An asset class, consisting of land and structures on that land, that requires far more expertise for success than most people realize. While seemingly a generic investment, real estate varies tremendously across geographies and uses of land and buildings. Skilled real estate investors in one type or location seldom can translate that skill to other widely separated locations or types. Those seeking to invest in real estate through established developers are apt to be disappointed since the best developers seldom need additional outside investment to bring their projects to fruition, their reputation and the development itself serving as collateral for the necessary borrowings.

Recession—Traditionally defined as two consecutive quarters of negative economic growth as measured by GDP. In recent years recessions that afflicted the entire U.S. economy have been replaced by "rolling recessions," which affect only one or a few industries at any time, such as the domestic automobile industry, which shrank severely during the otherwise healthy economic growth of the past few years, followed in 2007 by the housing industry. Rolling recessions are easier to counter than general recessions since more resources can be focused on the affected industry. Recessions in either form, while causing pain for those experiencing them, have the salutary effect of leading to new ways of doing things and new products that eventually lead to stronger economic growth.

Return—That which results from investing, whether it be monetary gains or knowledge that can be applied to future situations, measured in myriad ways, including before and after taxes and over different time spans. The returns on two investments that each double in value can be very different if one occurs over one year and the other occurs over ten years, the first being extremely unlikely to continue for more than one or two years, the latter being well within the range of historical values.

Reward—That which results from investing that includes not only the return, usually measured mathematically, but also the psychological benefits. Some investments—vacations, second homes, and boats, for example—may result in monetary losses over time that are more than offset by psychological rewards.

Risk—The penalty for being wrong, wrong being defined as an outcome that prevents the investor from accomplishing goals.

Securities analyst—The job of a securities analyst, like Julius Caesar's generals, is to never be surprised, even though it took them three days to bury their dead. An analyst pores over the relevant published data on a company, industry, sector, market, and economy to come up with a range of scenarios, some of which are most likely and others that would only occur if something out of the ordinary happens. Additional color is sought from suppliers, competitors, customers, regulators, former employees (particularly unhappy ones), and occasionally management. All of these elements are secondary to price. Any company that is likely to survive is a great bargain at a given low price, and a disaster about to happen at a popular high price. The best analysts, like the best field commanders, are often lonely since most observers fail to see what they see. As with most of investing, long-term success is an art form dependent upon surviving and finding and keeping some clients. An understanding home life is a big plus. Some analysts can become good portfolio managers by learning additional skills and broadening their basic knowledge. Not all good analysts make good portfolio managers, and there should be a fulfilling career role for them.

Speculation—When Bernard (Bernie) Baruch, an advisor to a number of presidents and a friend of my grandfather's, was testifying before the U.S. Congress, he was asked in a derogatory tone if he was a speculator. Yes, he said, then explained the derivation of the word. *Speculate* comes from the Latin that means "so see far ahead." He was often quoted that one should buy straw (summer) hats in the winter when their prices were low, speculating that there would be a bigger demand in the summer in those pre-air-conditioning days. A speculator is essentially someone who sees future change and is focused more on the future than on the current environment. Speculators can be wrong both in their perceived future and its time of arrival. The mere act of speculation may be like the uncertainty principle in atomic physics in that the examination and pronouncement could cause the speculation to become more accepted or even real. Certainly speculators take risks, but little is accomplished in society without some people who speculate about the future and act on their views.

Stock—A trading chip that everyone pretends represents a portion of ownership in a public company, but that is in reality a rental arrangement under which the shareholder temporarily shares in the fortunes of the company before trading that chip for something else that seems to have better prospects.

Taxes—At the most fundamental level, the cost imposed on you by others for the privilege of living among them. More pointedly, taxes are the world's worst form of asset allocation given that politicians decide how to apportion your money. While many regard the U.S. government as among the world's worst asset allocators, certain state governments make the federal government look like an investment genius.

Trading—Regularly buying and selling. Successful trading is much more an art form than a science. The better traders have at least equivalent knowledge about current facts, trends, and rumors as anyone else. Many traders are equipped with a well-developed instinct about how the markets will evolve in the short term. If one is new to the game, it is best not to play with professionals unless one can afford an expensive lesson.

Trust—A document used to give money to someone in return for accepting the grantor's orders and values whether the grantor is dead or alive.

Value—Like pornography and beauty, value is in the eyes of the beholder. Too often investors assess value by comparing the price of a security today with prices of perceived peers that are publicly or privately traded. This approach is called the arbitrage theory of pricing and is central to many analysts' pricing models. Unfortunately the peers may also be mispriced. Another, and more difficult, method would be to project the sum total of all future dividends for an extended time plus a terminal price for the stock discounted for the probability of obtaining these results. The approximate range of the discount to be applied is from the current long-term U.S. Treasury bond yield for something that is certain, to twice the current yield on an index of "junk" bonds or high-current-yield funds for the very uncertain.

Value in a public company is created by management's ability to effectively marshal and deploy assets, including people, to produce profits in the face of competition. That being said, Warren Buffett cautions us that value lies first and foremost in the nature of the business. Good management will always lose to a good business.

Venture capital—An investment market that differs from horse racing in that most horses will finish a given race while more than a few venture-capital investments will simply disappear, the result of bankruptcy, extreme dilution, mismanagement, or, on occasion, fraud. A successful venture-capital investment can produce returns on the order of fifty to a hundred times the original investment, but those gains are often offset by losses on many other venture-capital investments. Contrary to common belief, most start-ups are not funded by venture capital, but by angel investors, vendor financing, and other techniques.

Volatility—A measure of how bouncy the ride is along a road or trend line measured by the distance above and below the best fitted straight line through the region of the observations. The amplitude of the swings above and below the trend is called the standard deviation, which has nothing to do with morals or the risk of large losses.

Wealth—The condition of having more assets than one needs to live a satisfactory life, regardless of the amount of assets.

Will—A document that is not a statement of love. Rather it is a statement of the will maker's philosophy that becomes, upon his or her death, a declaration of familial war since it almost never satisfies everyone. Fortunately, the decedent doesn't care.

✦ APPENDIX ✦

Introduction to the
Dow Jones Industrial Average (DJIA)

Throughout this book, we have used the Dow Jones Industrial Average for comparison purposes. What follows is a brief look at the shifting stocks included in the DJIA at the beginning of each decade, plus an opportunity for readers to generate their suggested components of the 2010 index.

The reasons that stocks enter and leave the index can briefly be summarized as follows:

1. In 1896 when the index began, just twelve stocks were in the index, and that number, but not the names, remained constant until the decade beginning with 1920.
2. For the next ten years the index was expanded to twenty.
3. In the next decade the number was increased to thirty, where it has remained to this day.

4. With no further expansion for at least eighty years, the only way for a new name to show up is for a stock to disappear from the index. For the most part stocks disappeared because they were acquired. In a limited number of cases the editors of *The Wall Street Journal* were fearful of an impending bankruptcy, for example Chrysler. In one case a name was dropped, only to return years later (IBM), because it was representing too big a portion of the index. (More on this in a moment.)

5. Replacement names were meant to be large companies that represented American industry and had a large following of investors that actively traded the stock. The term *industrials* was and is somewhat misleading if one thinks of smokestacks on top of factories that produce things. Even in its earliest days the industrial index included gas companies, and eventually AT&T was added, only to be replaced by one of its spin-offs, which eventually acquired its old parent. The index along the way picked up McDonald's and in the current decade two banks.

There are at least two other keys to understanding the index. The first is, as with the Standard & Poor's 500, the components are selected by a faceless group of employees of a publisher. Very few, even among professional investors, know the names of these decision makers. The second, and in many ways the most important, fact about an index that investors should know is how the index is calculated. In the case of the DJIA one must remember the original customers of the index were brokerage-house salesmen who needed instruments to encourage trading, not long-term investing. Thus, the index was price-weighted, with the stocks with the highest prices impacting the index more than their lower-priced brethren.

To use any index as a comparative tool, a wise investor needs to know about the selection process, calculation procedures, and the principal market that the publisher is targeting, plus the desirability of a derivative market based on the index. Dow Jones & Company for many years vigorously opposed anyone's trading their index for fear that any resulting loses could damage the company's image. Between the 1960s and when the company first authorized the use of their data for a derivative in the last perhaps ten years, two things happened. First a market opportunity was seized by McGraw-Hill to license the Standard & Poor indexes for the trading of derivatives. While the DJIA is the most well-known of all indexes and the public investor relates to its movement as the movement of the market, S&P dominates the institutional market and makes millions of dollars each year from its licenses. It had never been sued when the index dropped sharply. The other thing that happened were various attempts to create an almost gray market in trading/investment vehicles based on the performance of the DJIA. Some of these took the form of mutual funds. One of the earliest of these was in the late 1960s when my brother filed a prospectus with the SEC tightly modeled after the index. Later there were other fund attempts, none particularly successful. One other attempt is worth noting. In the mid-1980s, I was invited to go to Turkey to discuss the creation and marketing of money-market funds to a largely un-banked population. While there, I learned that in the local bazaar a closed group were trading their own version of the

DJIA. I was not permitted entry to that trading market. The lesson from all of this is that if there is sufficient demand, financial markets around the world will accommodate.

Take it from someone who has created both many individual stock indexes as well as fund indexes: you should understand any index before you attempt to use it effectively. The importance of really understanding the Dow Jones Industrial Average, or any index, is in its application as a comparative measure. When the DJIA produces a better return than your portfolio, it is not a sign that your portfolio is being invested badly. Performance gaps should not be used to provide excuses for firing the manager, including yourself, but for beginning a series of evolving questions. Often the very components can be priced too high relative to the general price level in the market, which can be a cause for concern. For most investors, there should be a difference between the index and your account. The index was never designed to be a prudent account. The index does not carry any transaction costs, administrative expenses, or underinvested cash. None of the popular indexes are actually audited by CPA firms. To some degree the audit and expense questions are dealt with in using Exchange Traded Funds based on the full replication of an index.

The Original Components of the Dow Jones Industrial Average in 1896

American Cotton Oil

American Sugar

American Tobacco

Chicago Gas
Distilling & Cattle Feeding
General Electric
Laclede Gas
National Lead
North American
Tennessee Coal & Iron
U.S. Leather pfd.
U.S. Rubber

The DJIA in 1900

American Cotton Oil
American Steel & Wire
American Sugar
Continental Tobacco
Federal Steel
General Electric Company
National Lead
Pacific Mail Steamship
Peoples Gas
Tennessee Coal & Iron
U.S. Leather pfd.
U.S. Rubber

The DJIA in 1910

Amalgamated Copper
American Car & Foundry

American Smelting & Refining

American Sugar

Colorado Fuel & Iron

General Electric Company

National Lead

Peoples Gas

U.S. Rubber

U.S. Rubber first pfd.

U.S. Steel

U.S. Steel pfd.

The DJIA in 1920

American Can

American Car & Foundry

American Locomotive

American Smelting

American Sugar

American Telephone & Telegraph

Anaconda Copper

Baldwin Locomotive

Central Leather

Corn Products

General Electric Company

Goodrich

Republic Iron & Steel

Studebaker

Texas Company

U.S. Rubber

U.S. Steel
Utah Copper
Western Union
Westinghouse

The DJIA in 1930

Allied Chemical
American Can
American Smelting
American Sugar
American Tobacco B
Atlantic Refining
Bethlehem Steel
Chrysler
Curtiss-Wright
General Electric Company
General Foods
General Motors Corporation
General Railway Signal
Goodrich
International Harvester
International Nickel
Mack Truck
Nash Motors
National Cash Register
Paramount Publix
Radio Corporation
Sears Roebuck & Company

Standard Oil (N.J.)

Texas Company

Texas Gulf Sulphur

Union Carbide

U.S. Steel

Westinghouse Electric

Woolworth

The DJIA in 1940

Allied Chemical

American Can

American Smelting

American Telephone & Telegraph

American Tobacco B

Bethlehem Steel

Chrysler

Corn Products Refining

Du Pont

Eastman Kodak Company

General Electric Company

General Foods

General Motors Corporation

Goodyear

International Harvester

International Nickel

Johns-Manville

Loew's

National Distillers

National Steel

Procter & Gamble Company

Sears Roebuck & Company

Standard Oil (N.J.)

Standard Oil of California

Texas Company

Union Carbide

United Aircraft

U.S. Steel

Westinghouse Electric

Woolworth

The DJIA in 1950 (no changes from 1940)

Allied Chemical

American Can

American Smelting

American Telephone & Telegraph

American Tobacco B

Bethlehem Steel

Chrysler

Corn Products Refining

Du Pont

Eastman Kodak Company

General Electric Company

General Foods

General Motors Corporation

Goodyear

International Harvester

International Nickel
Johns-Manville
Loew's
National Distillers
National Steel
Procter & Gamble Company
Sears Roebuck & Company
Standard Oil (N.J.)
Standard Oil of California
Texas Company
Union Carbide
United Aircraft
U.S. Steel
Westinghouse Electric
Woolworth

The DJIA in 1960

Allied Chemical
Aluminum Company of America
American Can
American Telephone & Telegraph
American Tobacco B
Anaconda Copper
Bethlehem Steel
Chrysler
Du Pont
Eastman Kodak Company
General Electric Company

General Foods
General Motors Corporation
Goodyear
International Harvester
International Nickel
International Paper Company
Johns-Manville
Owens-Illinois Glass
Procter & Gamble Company
Sears Roebuck & Company
Standard Oil (N.J.)
Standard Oil of California
Swift & Company
Texaco, Inc.
Union Carbide
United Aircraft
U.S. Steel
Westinghouse Electric
Woolworth

The DJIA in 1970 (no change from 1960)

Allied Chemical
Aluminum Company of America
American Can
American Telephone & Telegraph
American Tobacco B
Anaconda Copper
Bethlehem Steel

Chrysler

Du Pont

Eastman Kodak Company

General Electric Company

General Foods

General Motors Corporation

Goodyear

International Harvester

International Nickel

International Paper Company

Johns-Manville

Owens-Illinois Glass

Procter & Gamble Company

Sears Roebuck & Company

Standard Oil (N.J.)

Standard Oil of California

Swift & Company

Texaco, Inc.

Union Carbide

United Aircraft

U.S. Steel

Westinghouse Electric

Woolworth

The DJIA in 1980

Allied Chemical

Aluminum Company of America

American Can
American Telephone & Telegraph
American Tobacco B
Bethlehem Steel
Du Pont
Eastman Kodak Company
Exxon Corporation
General Electric Company
General Foods
General Motors Corporation
Goodyear
Inco
International Business Machines
International Harvester
International Paper Company
Johns-Manville
Merck & Company, Inc.
Minnesota Mining & Manufacturing
Owens-Illinois Glass
Procter & Gamble Company
Sears Roebuck & Company
Standard Oil of California
Texaco Incorporated
Union Carbide
United Technologies Corporation
U.S. Steel
Westinghouse Electric
Woolworth

The DJIA in 1990

Allied-Signal, Inc.

Aluminum Company of America

American Express Company

American Telephone & Telegraph

Bethlehem Steel

Boeing Company

Chevron

Coca-Cola Company

Du Pont

Eastman Kodak Company

Exxon Corporation

General Electric Company

General Motors Corporation

Goodyear

International Business Machines

International Paper Company

McDonald's Corporation

Merck & Company, Inc.

Minnesota Mining & Manufacturing

Navistar International Corp.

Philip Morris Companies, Inc.

Primerica Corporation

Procter & Gamble Company

Sears Roebuck & Company

Texaco Incorporated

Union Carbide

United Technologies Corporation

USX Corporation
Westinghouse Electric
Woolworth

The DJIA in 2000

Alcoa, Inc.
Allied-Signal, Inc.
American Express Company
AT&T Corporation
Boeing Company
Caterpillar, Inc.
Citigroup, Inc.
Coca-Cola Company
Du Pont
Eastman Kodak Company
Exxon Corporation
General Electric Company
General Motors Corporation
Hewlett-Packard Company
Home Depot, Inc.
Intel Corporation
International Business Machines
International Paper Company
Johnson & Johnson
J. P. Morgan & Company
McDonald's Corporation
Merck & Company, Inc.
Microsoft Corporation

Minnesota Mining & Manufacturing

Philip Morris Companies, Inc.

Procter & Gamble Company

SBC Communications, Inc.

United Technologies Corporation

Wal-Mart Stores, Inc.

Walt Disney Company

Current Components of the DJIA

3M Company

Alcoa, Inc.

Altria Group, Inc.

American Express Company

American International Group

AT&T Incorporated

Boeing Corporation

Caterpillar, Inc.

Citigroup Incorporated

Coca-Cola Company

Du Pont

Exxon Mobil Corporation

General Electric Company

General Motors Corporation

Hewlett-Packard Company

Home Depot, Inc.

Honeywell International, Inc.

Intel Corporation

International Business Machines

Johnson & Johnson

J. P. Morgan Chase & Company

McDonald's Corporation

Merck & Company, Inc.

Microsoft Corporation

Pfizer, Inc.

Procter & Gamble Company

United Technologies

Verizon Company

Wal-Mart Stores, Inc.

Walt Disney Company

The DJIA in 2010

(Make your own list.)

✦ INDEX ✦

Index

Index